RUNNING UP HILLS

AN IRREVERENT JOURNEY
THROUGH THE UPS AND DOWNS OF LIFE
(or...The Cynical Ramblings of a Sixty-Something Bloke)

PAUL WESTON

©2024 Paul Weston
Running Up Hills – An Irreverent Journey Through the Ups and Downs of Life.

eBook ISBN: 978-1-962570-88-6
Paperback ISBN: 978-1-962570-86-2
Ingram Spark ISBN: 978-1-962570-87-9

Editor: Susan Crossman
Cover Image: Adobe Stock
Cover Design: Angela Ayala
Interior Design: Marigold2k
Publisher: Spotlight Publishing House – Goodyear, AZ
https://spotlightpublishinghouse.com

ALL RIGHTS RESERVED. No part of this book may be reproduced or transmitted in any form or by any means, electronic, mechanical, photocopying, recording or by any information storage or retrieval system, for public or private use without prior written permission of the author, except in the case of brief quotations embodied in articles and reviews.

www.paulwestonconsulting.com

RUNNING UP HILLS

AN IRREVERENT JOURNEY THROUGH THE UPS AND DOWNS OF LIFE
(or...The Cynical Ramblings of a Sixty-Something Bloke)

PAUL WESTON

SPOTLIGHT
PUBLISHING HOUSE

Goodyear, Arizona

Table of Contents

Introduction ix
Chapter 1   A Hill Called Faff 1
Chapter 2   A Hill Called Lost Luggage 15
Chapter 3   A Hill Called Packaging 35
Chapter 4   A Hill Called Jobsworth 53
Chapter 5   A Hill Called Passion (in Sports) 71
Chapter 6   A Hill Called Sporting Cheats 91
Chapter 7   A Hill Called Alzheimer's 113
Chapter 8   A Hill Called Tourette 125
Chapter 9   Getting to the Top 147
Acknowledgments 151
About the Author 153

For the "Old Fella"—forever on a hill!

Introduction

Running in the Rain may not be the most pleasant activity to start your day, but if you want a distraction from the soaking wet feet, clingy clothes and soggy hat on your head, then plan a route that means you have to run up a hill. Because if it is steep enough, then being wet will pale into insignificance, and the rain will be the least of your worries.

And as with running in the rain, if you do run up a few hills, the feeling of accomplishment will make you feel a lot better about life than just jogging along a flat road in the dry. If you are lucky enough to live in the right place, the hill you run up may have some sheep on it, which I think would be great, because sheep have always been creatures of interest to me.

They lead a life so simple I sometimes wonder: if I were to have my time again, would I want to come back as one? They certainly don't seem to be bothered by many of the things we allow into our minds—like rain... and hills.

But right now, I was dealing with both.

It was pissing down with rain, and I was halfway up a very, very steep hill. Winnats Pass is a limestone gorge in the Peak District of Derbyshire, England. The name is a corruption of "wind gates" due to the winds swirling through the pass. It lies west of the village of Castleton, in the National Trust's High Peak Estate and the High Peak borough of Derbyshire. It is very steep, to the point of a 28% incline in some places (if you aren't familiar with this form of hill gradient, it feels like you are running up a wall), and has, on occasion, been selected for the British Cycling National Hill Climb Championships because the ascent is so severe.

My parents lived a few miles from Castleton in a village called Bradwell, and that morning I was out for a fifteen-kilometre run in very typical Derbyshire weather: rain and strong winds.

While Winnats Pass is technically only around one-and-a-half kilometers long, starting from the lowest point in the area—the river running through the centre of Castleton—adds another one-and-a-half kilometers to the jaunt through the pass. The gradient out of Castleton is also pretty intense but is nothing like the steepest parts of Winnats.

I had already run from Bradwell that morning and had been on the road for around thirty minutes by the time I passed over the river and started the long climb. And I was wet.

Very wet.

So wet that *everything* I was wearing was totally soaked.

And I was loving it.

But once I started up the winding footpath that ran parallel to the road where cars were struggling not to burn out clutches on the way up or brakes on the way down, I wasn't thinking about the weather any longer anyway. Instead, my focus was on maintaining my pace and upward progress, because once you stop, it becomes very hard to get going again—and, also, my heartbeat, which seemed dangerously close to cardiac arrest territory, was pounding in my ears to the point I thought it was vying for headspace with my brain.

The pass winds upwards around limestone rock, and it is impossible to see the summit as you ascend. Gauging my progress and assessing how far there was to go was made even more difficult by the low cloud shrouding the top, so my only option was to keep blowing and keep going.

But at least I wasn't alone, because watching me suffer in the rain were several dozen sheep. They weren't blowing, they were mostly chewing on the plentiful supply of grass, and urinating and excreting at will. What a life they led. An endless supply of all the food they would ever want, no need to line up for the bathroom, and no need to be shy about their bodily functions. As I slowly made my way upwards, a couple of sheep stared at me with what looked like a mixture of caution and question.

Was I a threat to them? And what was I doing out here in the rain when I had a nice warm house to stay in? In case I was a threat, some of them decided to take evasive action. They turned around and skipped hurriedly up the steep grassy bank to my right. Others meandered out onto the road to be greeted with a screeching of brakes or grinding of gears as drivers took evasive action.

And one turned away from me, spread her back legs wide apart and emptied the contents of her bladder in my direction.

Sheep are not known for their general intelligence: their brain size is proportionately smaller than a human's (although I can think of a few people whose behaviour would challenge that theory). But what they lack in intellect, they make up for in resilience in the face of both weather and terrain. They get into the most obscure locations you can imagine.

There have been times when I have reached the top of a remote mountain, or the extremities of a distant objective on a trek or expedition and thought there couldn't possibly be another living creature for miles… only to hear a familiar "bhaa, bhaa," and the emergence from the mist of a sheep or two.

Almost nothing stops them.

They see hills as part of life.

They rarely avoid them and, in fact, use them as an escape from the threats created by we humans.

For sheep, hills are a good thing.

For me... well, the physical hills I run up as part of my training certainly help me keep fit. But what about the mental hills we face in our lives? You know, the stuff that annoys us.

That is irritating.

That raises the blood pressure.

That makes us moan.

That maybe stops us doing stuff we want to do.

Well, these are the hills we're going to spend a bit of time running up in these pages.

But as a word of caution, this is not a "self-help" book... in fact, by the time you get to the end, you may well need to buy one of those (sorry).

We're going to explore some of the areas that, during my life, have annoyed me. Irritated me.

Raised my blood pressure.

And almost made me stop doing stuff I wanted to do. But I also think you will share my feelings. You may well nod your head and think "yep, I know where he's coming from."

So, what hills are we up against?

Well, I'll start by introducing you to the concept of faffing.

We'll look at the agony of an airline losing your bag.

We'll discuss the frustration of packaging and how it once nearly got me arrested.

We'll open the topic of jobsworths and how they impact our lives.

We'll consider the pain that comes with being passionate about sport.

We'll dig into the sad world of the sporting cheat.

And we'll tackle two of the most challenging hills I have come across in my life: my mother's fight with Alzheimer's disease and my own journey of living with Tourette Syndrome.

I hope this all offers you a chance to consider the hills in your life.

I hope what I will share will offer you an opportunity for personal reflection.

And I hope you find the upward journey on which we are about to embark to be relevant, enlightening… and just maybe a bit of fun.

Paul Weston
July 2024

CHAPTER 1

A Hill Called Faff

The flight had already been delayed by more than eight hours. Tempers were becoming ever-more frayed with each added minute, but at last we were finally boarding.

The "Zone 2" written on my Boarding Pass meant I wasn't amongst the first group on the aircraft, but I was close enough to beat the mass rush in the main cabin. The aircraft was an Airbus A220 with three seats on one side of the aisle and two on the other. As I stepped through the door and turned right to find my seat, I faced a bottleneck of people. The stoppage was caused by a middle-aged woman who had decided that in order to get comfortable in her seat, needed to not only empty most of the contents of her carry-on luggage, but also rearrange what appeared to be 90% of her life's possessions.

Laptop, vanity case, books (three), magazine, pillow, blanket, socks, neck cushion (which also required inflating; it took four attempts to insert the stop valve). There then followed a full disinfecting procedure of her seat, headrest, pull-down tray and armrests before her first attempt to put her luggage in the overhead compartment, which ultimately failed because even though it appeared most of the contents were strewn around her seat, the bag was still too heavy to lift. Her second attempt gained assistance from the passenger most immediately behind her if for no other reason than that he looked likely to resort to physical violence if she didn't sit down within the next ten seconds.

And so the line started to move again and I got to my seat, moved out of the aisle to allow others to pass, withdrew my laptop and book from my bag, then placed it in the overhead compartment and sat down, only to discover the line had stopped again as the aforementioned woman was once again back on her feet and digging into her bag for yet more equipment. Out came her laptop power cable, phone charger, alternate shoes, hand cream, headphones, and a sleep mask (this was only a three-hour flight—it's not like we were the first manned flight to Mars or anything).

As she sat down again, the line of passengers began moving forward and my eyes gently settled on her to see what was next on the agenda. But one word raised its head in my mind and sent my psychological early warning system into overdrive… FAFFER.

The flight departed and the drama continued. Up and down to her bag. Ordering food from the flight attendants but not having her credit card ready, digging into her bag to find it… again. A constant routine of book changing, alternate clothing options—up and down, up and down.

And then we got to the arrival chapter of the drama.

Once the wheels were on the ground, the lady's phone was switched on and a loud conversation with her best friend forever/sister/confidante ensued about the status of her life at that time, the recent dating conquests (mostly failed by all accounts), the condition of her mother's arthritis, and a review of her hairstyle options. We reached the gate, the seatbelt sign turned off and preparations for disembarking began for most of us—but not the faffer.

Oh no, rather than get her stuff together, the phone call continued until all passengers in front of her had left the aircraft, at which point she stood up to block the aisle, pushed the phone into the crook of her neck so she could continue the call, and started the process of closing down her laptop, winding up the charging cable, unplugging and winding up her phone charger, putting her shoes back on (after swapping her socks), deflating her neck cushion, rolling it up and putting it back in the bag.

She required help from the passenger behind her to recover her carry-on suitcase from the overhead compartment and, once it was on her seat, began to completely repack all its contents while still managing to advise her best friend forever/sister/confidante on what she should be planting in her garden that spring.

As we were now in a much colder climate than the one from which we had departed, a jacket had to be worn, a scarf found and wrapped tightly around the neck (though judging by the comments from passengers behind me, it could never be tight enough), gloves recovered from the depths of her bag and then, finally, she was on the move.

We had left the aircraft and started to walk up the gate ramp when once again we came to a halt. Another blockage, accompanied by a familiar voice up front as the faffer, with shoulders hunched over her phone, looked at her calendar while trying to find a suitable date for lunch with best friend forever/sister/confidante.

No Time for Patience

As I get older, I seem to suffer from a distinct lack of patience. No, allow me to rephrase that. As I get older, I seem to suffer from *even less* patience than I had when I was younger.

If there is one quality I have adopted from my father (and he has many) it is the ability not to mess around and instead get on with things. If there was a job that needed doing around the house or garden, he would get it done—then. Not later in the day. Not the next day, week or month. But then.

And another of his qualities (or I should probably rephrase that as a quirk), was his lack of patience with "faffers."

The faffer is quite simply someone who dithers around. Who appears to lack the basics of focus. Who seems incapable of taking immediate action in a forthright manner and instead faffs around doing menial tasks of no importance or value, often resulting in a total abdication of the completion of projects or even the simplest task of being somewhere on time.

You may ask why I would allow a faffer to get to me. To live rent-free in my mind. To bother me if it is they who must deal with the consequences.

Well, as with all of us, there are faffers who take so long to complete the simplest of tasks they can have significant impact on our own efficiency: they aren't ready on time, they don't finish the washing up so someone else can use the kitchen, they don't get the shopping list ready so we can leave the house in enough time to beat the traffic.

Have you ever been a bit tight for time but needed to collect some groceries and found as you were standing in the checkout line there is someone in front of you who takes forever to load the belt, after which they chat with the checkout person, fail to pack the produce into bags as their groceries are scanned, and instead allow for a build-up which reaches back to your own grocery items? They then keep chatting while idly trying to find a method of payment, before which they remember they have some vouchers to redeem and, also, want to apply a price check to an apple, saving them, at most, a penny.

But is this faffing, or just bad organization? Well, one can be a symptom of the other: these people may be badly organized because they faff a lot. Or perhaps they are badly organized, and then fall prey to faffing. Is it just laziness or does the perennial faffer have a serious problem, possibly requiring medical assistance?

Some faffers are what we might call 'lightweights' in that they have the occasional tendency to become distracted at times. They are almost always productive. They get stuff done, are reliable and care about the people in their lives who rely on them. To these people, the odd period of faffing makes little difference. In fact (as will be shared below), it can be quite healthy to have a reasonable faff now and then as it makes them feel like they are entering the world of the rogue, the world of the efficiency miscreant. They share a little inward smile to themselves as the crown of consistent effectiveness in their lives slips to a gentle angle of jauntiness. It may be a day off work or a weekend when they may have had plans to complete a number of seemingly important tasks but, instead, are consumed by faffiness and potter from insignificant activity to insignificant activity.

But who cares?

They only have to push the "GO" button and they will start the engine of productivity and get things moving again.

If only.

For the lightweights, for whom faffing is basically just a quick battery recharge, it can be a nice break from the constant grind of efficient productivity. A reset back to a quiet life, undisturbed by a conscience that holds you accountable for being "on the go" from waking to sleeping. A light faff can be invigorating. It can give them a sample of how lesser mortals live. How the less focused spend their lives. They may even feel the freshness of not caring about stuff that is always on their mind. But at some point, the whole house of cards will likely come tumbling down when the realization of delaying any longer on a task or chore hits them full in the face, and the guilt of the casual faffer consumes their day.

There's More Than One

There are also categories within the faffer family.

Firstly, we have the *purists*. They subconsciously set themselves high standards in most areas of their lives. They like to plan, plan and plan again. They generally worry about any tiny eventuality (realistic, or, more likely, imagined) and they need to create a strategy with Critical Success Factors and Barriers assessed and formalized in greater depth than it took to land a man on the moon.

I once worked with a colleague who typified this group. She was constantly late with projects and kept everyone in her team on edge with her endless adding of tasks to evidently simple strategies. She had the ability to destroy meetings during which the rest of us reached a perfectly acceptable solution to a problem within a few minutes, only to spend the next forty-five listening to her making it as complicated as possible. She was also single, and, according to her girlfriends, hardly ever went on dates because she was so ultra particular about the prospects who kept popping up in her dating apps.

Next, we have the *kitten-syndromers*. This group live their lives amongst almost total distraction. They have good intent to get on with things, but the slightest little event that pops up in their lives (text, email, Slack message) is enough to take them away for hours at a time. They have the attention span of very young kittens: anything and everything can and does usually take them away from their daily chores. They have little appreciation of how long it will take to accomplish tasks and take on way, way, way more than they can possibly hope to achieve in the time available.

And, finally, we have the *any-excusers*. This lot are masters at finding reasons to NOT do something. Be it cleaning the house (it doesn't really need it), cutting the grass (it might rain today) doing their laundry (I can get another month out this underwear) or cooking a proper meal (why do I have a microwave if I'm not going to buy ready-made meals?).

Instead, they fill their days with pointless activities that create little or no value, and yet still create the impression the day has been fulfilling. There is a whole difference between being *active* and being *productive*—but not to your average faffer.

As with most activities (or lack thereof) there is a counter-opinion, and my research into the world of faffing led me to a piece by Tom Hodgkinson, who as editor of the magazine *The Idler* claims:

> *Faffing is good. It is an important part of life. Faffing is when we disconnect from the matrix and idle for a while, like a car. Our body and spirit know deep down that human beings were not made for constant toil so subconsciously creates space through the mechanism of faffing.*[1]

The Idler is a bi-monthly magazine, devoted to its ethos of "idling." On this practice, Hodgkinson writes:

> *A characteristic of the idler's work is that it looks suspiciously like play. This, again, makes the non-idler feel uncomfortable. Victims of the Protestant work ethic would like all work to be unpleasant. They feel that work is a curse, that we must suffer on this earth to earn our place in the next. The idler, on the other hand, sees no reason not to use his brain to organise a life for himself where his play is his work, and so attempt to create his own little paradise in the here and now.*[2]

I can think of a lot of people who would worship the Idler's Messiah that is Tom Hodgkinson for presenting these views, as it gives them an excuse for lack of productivity. It allows them to poke fun at those of us who live in the *hamster wheel of continual work and general "busy-ness."* They can sit back, relaxing in the knowledge that they are no longer alone in this world of sedentary faffing, not worrying whether they get somewhere on time (if they even get there at all).

---

[1] Source: https://www.brainyquote.com/quotes/tom_hodgkinson_527563
[2] Source: https://www.brainyquote.com/quotes/tom_hodgkinson_527563

And as for running up the hill called faff. Well, the hill is something best left alone. It doesn't matter what is at the top. Who cares anyway? Stay on the flat, or better still, don't even leave the house in the first place.

We're All Guilty M'Lord

So, can a highly productive and active person submit to faffing?

Well, when I looked deep inside myself, I did indeed discover the inner faffer lying there in the thick murkiness of my psyche. It looked up from the depths and smiled one of those Jack Nicholson, "Here's Johnny" smiles that said, "I'm here and I can take you over whenever I want."

And it does. In my case it is generally related to tendencies leaning towards Obsessive Compulsive Disorder (OCD) and a fundamental paranoia over forgetting something I need for a trip, leaving a light on, going to bed with the garage door open or failing to lock the car.

International business travel has played a significant part in my professional career since leaving the military in my early forties. Trips are usually planned several months in advance and my countdown to departure day will include the forming of a "kit pile" of what I will take with me from a few days out. I learned a long time ago that restricting my bags to carry-on only is a life-changing experience, so contents will only include specific business clothes I will take with me to ensure I do not wear them a day or so before departure and they therefore stay clean. I always like to run wherever I go, so that attire is set aside, as are the documents and technical equipment (laptop, cables, PowerPoint clickers, speaking notes etc.) I will need. Of course, some of it I will be using right up to the moment I leave, so I will list them on a paper which is placed on my bag to ensure I check them off as I zip up and ready myself on the day.

This would include my passport and any Visas and other travel documents.

Now. I will have made a list of what needs to be taken with me. I will pack what I can well in advance. I will pack the remainder as I finish using it and only have to add the final items on the morning of travel. But the night before, I have been known to completely unpack my bag and recheck every item. I will place my passport in a specific pocket on my bag and leave the bag close to the door to the garage the night before I travel.

The passport is *in* the bag. I put it there the night before. There is no way it can *possibly* be anywhere else, and yet I have also been known to get twenty minutes into the drive to the airport and have had to pull over to the side of the road to ensure I do indeed have it with me.

Faffing? Certainly, the eve-of-travel bag repack is an unnecessary activity that probably qualifies, but I would claim the highway stop and check is more about OCD than anything else.

But, I hear you ask, what possible damage can someone else's faffing have on us?

In my case I once witnessed an example so severe I was close to physical assault.

As any long-distance runner will tell you, if you run for long enough, you are likely to get black toenails, usually on the toe next to your big toe. These are usually caused by the nail rubbing against your running shoe, which causes a blister under the nail, which then turns black. They aren't particularly serious, and don't usually cause too much discomfort, but after three years of training for and racing in endurance events, I found, during heavy training periods, the second nail on my right foot was becoming very enlarged with a huge blister beneath it. Indeed, after my first Ironman triathlon, the under-toe blister was so bad that when I came to finally burst it, even though my foot was on the bathroom counter next to the sink, the explosion of blister content reached the ceiling.

I decided to visit a podiatrist who proposed I have the nail removed and the roots burned out so they would not return, which at the time seemed a logical and totally reasonable proposition. On the day of my procedure, I was asked to sit in a chair, remove my shoe and sock, and put my right foot on a surgical tray. A screen separated me from the podiatrist and as we got underway, he explained he was first going to anaesthetize my toe (no kidding). While the screen was there to stop me from watching the proceedings, I could see most of the preparation that was taking place, and at that moment was very keen for him to just stick the needle in and be done with the painful bit.

But this guy was a talker.

After "scrubbing up" and getting his Personal Protective Equipment on, he asked me what I liked to do with my time? What had my weekend been like?

I do triathlons and the weekend was fine—just stick the needle in.

He asked me how long I had been in Canada and what part of Australia was I from?

Fifteen years and I'm English—just stick the needle in.

He asked me what I thought of the Canadian winters and had I taken up [ice] hockey?

Cold and I'm hopeless at [ice] hockey—just stick the needle in.

He eventually put the needle into the bottle of anaesthetic and withdrew into the syringe the requisite amount—I was now, at last, ready—but no, he had the wrong glasses on, so put the cover back on the needle, placed it on the tray, pulled off his surgical gloves and left the room in search of the right pair.

On his return, and after another hand scrubbing session, he was back in place to get going—at last.

But not before more questions.

Did I see the Leafs' game last night and did I think they were going to miss the playoffs again?

I don't follow hockey—just stick the needle in.

Did I live locally and how often do I get back to Australia?

Yes, I live close by, and once again, I'm ENGLISH—just stick the needle in.

He then pulled the cover off the needle, leaned forward ready to strike... then sat up again and asked me if I'd tried the new Thai Restaurant next to his offices?

JUST... STICK... THE... NEEDLE... IN!

When Faffing is Par for the Course

Now, if ever there is a sport that attracts faffers, it has to be golf, particularly in North America. As someone who grew up learning the game amongst some of the oldest and most traditional clubs in England, etiquette and respect for fellow golfers became part of my golfing DNA. We were taught that a decent round should be completed in around three hours, as long as everyone does their bit to keep things moving. Simple routines such as being aware of who has the "honour" on each tee and consequently plays first, then directly marking their scorecard from the previous hole rather than reviewing each and every shot, noting how the wind affected their drive, commenting on how the lake in front of the green is longer than it says on the card, complaining that the yardage markers are not accurate and the green is not consistent with the others... these are all debates to be had in the clubhouse bar.

While waiting for the group in front to move up the fairway or clear the green, you are taught to select your club, take your practice swings and be ready to play as soon as the coast is clear. As you walk up to the green, you take note of where the next tee is and place your bag in an appropriate place, so you are able to take the most direct route to collect it from flag to tee once done on the current hole.

If you land in a bunker, you grab the rake before you play and place it close by, so on completion of your next shot you are ready to rake the sand smooth rather than having to head off in search of said gardening tool.

On the green you start lining up your putt while your partners are playing, ensuring you are all set when it is your turn.

And as soon as you have all "holed-out" you replace the flag and move off to the next tee with the player whose honour it is ready to drive immediately if the fairway is clear.

The other added benefit in the days of my golf "training" was the almost total absence of golf carts—those open-plan roofed vehicles that transport players around the course while convincing overweight golfers they are actually getting some exercise. My cart theory may seem counterintuitive to my rationale around faster golf: after all, surely having some form of vehicular support will get you around the course quicker.

But does it?

Each cart generally carries two players, so you have to drive to two balls, which is okay if they land close to each other, but if they don't (and they rarely do), then both players travel to one ball, the owner steps out, considers the distance for the next shot, goes through the drama of club selection, enjoys some practice swings, looks across the fairway to the other cart, usually starting a debate on who should go first (like it really matters—this isn't the Ryder Cup), then, at last, plays the shot, watches it pull, hook, slice or fade, cleans the club face with the rag attached to the cart, replaces it in the bag, climbs back into the cart, and drives across to the other passenger's ball (a distance of 75-100 yards or so in most cases—but still clearly too far to walk), where the whole faff is repeated by the other player.

But how is walking faster?

Well, for one thing, each player walks directly to their own ball, and while en route has the time to assess whose turn it will be to play first. Club selection is a task to be completed on the move, everyone gets ready to play when they are adjacent to their own ball and as soon as it is their turn—off they hit.

Once the ball is moving, clubs are wiped and bagged, and you are on the move again—directly to the next shot.

You can also walk anywhere on the course, whereas carts must stay away from green areas, often requiring golfers to park around the back and walk around again to the balls that may have landed short of the intended target. And, of course, there's the selection of wedges and putter which many golfers forget, resulting in an additional walk back to the cart.

Cart restrictions are also increased in the event of several days of inclement weather, meaning local rules ban them on any surface other than concrete, and golfers must drive them up the path adjacent to each fairway. Players must then walk across to their balls and back to the cart for every single shot. Add this drama to a right-handed player with a perennial fade/slice (the ball always flies right) when the compulsory cart path is up the left, and you have some long back-and-forths going on in front of you if you are in the group to the rear.

This sporting faff smacked me in the face when I became a resident of North America and after playing golf at a respectable pace for many decades on English courses, was stunned by how long it took to get around eighteen holes—in most cases well more than five hours.

Adding to the above faffing, there is the loading up of beer on the carts prior to starting out, then the arrival of the "refreshment" cart every few holes, where a replenishment of alcohol takes up additional time, while also adding to the frustration of golfers who are pretty average at best to start with.

And let's face it—if you aren't very good anyway, a few beers are not going to turn you into Jack Nicklaus, and yet the anger meter usually goes off the charts as drunken shots go ever more astray as the beers go down.

Then there is the golfer's hole-by-hole post-mortem that delays getting on with things even more: the shaking of the head, the expression of disbelief that the course could possibly treat them so badly, the utter disgust over the misfortune that has been bestowed upon them that day (and every day for some of those I have played with over the last few years).

Golf can be the great faffer's absolute comfort zone. The opportunities to do almost anything other than what you should be doing are almost eternal, and so if you are a compulsive faffer, and you are looking for an outlet for your passion, then golf could be the game for you.

Just make sure to let me know so I can stay home that day.

And so, when it comes to the hills in our life, the one named faff can be a tough climb, not only as a participant, but also as an observer for whom another's faffing can at times be intolerable. Yes, a good faff can be healthy for most of us—but whose life are you messing with if it takes you longer than a few seconds to sit your ass on an aircraft seat? But I also see so many people who miss out on activities they really want to enjoy because they faff around rather than getting on with things, and if that affects me and my life, then the hill becomes very steep.

CHAPTER 2

A Hill Called Lost Luggage

There is something rather transcendental about watching an airport baggage carousel go round and round and round.

Bags appear at the top of a belt ramp, get nudged to the side and then slide down onto the revolving bit to be collected by the lucky owners. As a traveller you start with a feeling of hope that increases when you arrive at your allocated carousel and, after a period of time, the warning siren sounds and the belt springs into life. Bags start to appear and if you are with a family member, you might plan a strategy: one of you grabs a trolley and stands to the rear, the other fights to the front to recover the luggage. Of course, this will likely resemble a combat mission as you fight through those families who set up a line of defence alongside the moving belt. You know what I mean: dad stands in the middle, mum is two paces to his right, the eldest son is two paces to his left, the other kids spread left and right, and if there are grandparents in tow, they are despatched to the wider flanks. They control the territory. This is *their patch*, and thou shall not pass, not even if *your* bag is there, ready for the taking.

But just seeing your bag appear is akin to winning the lottery. It signals success. You inwardly praise the airline for their professionalism and take back all the criticism you silently metered out over the last few hours of flight delays, awful food, crappy inflight entertainment and flight attendants who often appear to be so balanced they have a chip on both shoulders.

Does this sound like an exaggerated overreaction?

If you have never had an airline lose your bag, then you need to do more flying, because the other end of the bag carousel experience is standing there watching the number of bags slowly diminish, the exodus of happy smiling passengers heading for the exit, and, no matter how hard you stare at the top of that ramp, the realization that the end is nigh.

There are no more bags on the way.

The belt stops and I challenge even the most passive, rational, easy-going, relaxed and positive traveller to refrain from cursing their luck.

And so, it is off to "Baggage Services" where you join a lineup of people in the same situation as you: tired, frustrated, angry and generally pissed off.

If I were to name the top five jobs in the world I would not want to do, one of them would have to be working on the Baggage Services desk at an airport. I mean, some people treat you like it had been your job at the airport of departure to put their bag on the plane and you are expected to know exactly where the bag is and when it is going to be reunited with its owner.

I learned a long time ago that there is no point in getting angry (see Chapter 3): it could get you arrested. So, I have found that in-person interactions are best executed with politeness and respect, which is especially valuable if the passenger in front of you just exploded in a fit of rage.

But it can be tempting to just let it all out.

I have been very fortunate to have travelled to more than fifty countries in my life. I visited many of them during my military career, often embarked in a large grey steel warship travelling around the world at an average speed of fifteen miles per hour. But during my second career as a consultant and speaker, I have had the opportunity to do even more travel, certainly in more comfort, at a faster speed, but with less certainty that your bags are with you, because if you join a ship of the Royal Navy, unless you are the skipper, you carry your own bags over the gangway!

I've found that the more times you board an aircraft, the greater the chance your bags are staying put. For the first three years after I relocated my life to Canada in 2005, I only went back to the UK to attend family events, stay with my parents or go to reunions or memorial services. But in 2008, I had a business opportunity in Manchester, England, that meant I had to take appropriate clothing, so it was kind of critical that my bag arrive *with* me. Which is where Air Canada played their trump card for the first time.

The baggage claim at Heathrow is a sad and lonely place when you are looking in despair at an empty belt going round and round and round. This had never happened to me before. What to do? Well, off to Baggage Services and the back of a long line. At that time, one desk handled the lost luggage for all flights into Terminal 2, regardless of airline.

It was chaos.

The poor chap on duty that morning was swamped with flights from India, Pakistan, Egypt, South Africa, et al. And every airline had their own lost luggage procedures. After waiting in line for over an hour, it was finally my turn to report my loss, and all the duty staff member did was ask me to fill in a form with my flight details and forwarding address. I was told my bag would likely be put on the next flight, after which I was given a sheet of paper with a phone number I could call to learn where my bag was and when it was likely to arrive in the UK and, consequently, forwarded to my destination.

Now, this may *seem* simple.

I was staying at my parents' house in Derbyshire. The bag was in Toronto and would "likely" be put on the next flight. It should arrive the next day and be couriered to said address.

This was a Monday morning. I would be at my parents' house that afternoon. The meeting I had to be at in Manchester was on Wednesday afternoon. The bag should arrive on Tuesday morning and be at my parents later that afternoon. Plenty of time.

The bag contained my business suit, dress shirt, shoes and tie. I was standing up in an old pair of sweatpants, rugby shirt and a knackered pair of running shoes—not good for an important business meeting (although, if I were meeting with representatives of a tech company today it would probably be ideal).

Once I arrived at my parents' house, I got through the usual welcomes and then started the inquest into my bag.

Now, my mum had a serious habit of making bad situations worse, and rather than displaying optimism and hope, she kept stating how unlikely it was that my bag would arrive by Tuesday afternoon, in which case, what was I going to do? My dad, also not known for his eternal and forever uplifting positivity, set about sharing his thoughts on the state of the world today, how people don't give a crap any longer and for all the money they charge for flights you'd think they would be able to at least put a bag on an aircraft. But the trouble with my parents' approach was that it created in me a natural desire to defend Air Canada.

I'm also not known as a natural optimist. I've always been accused of being a pessimist when in fact I like to call it *realism* and, anyway, it's better to be pessimistic because if you are then wrong, you're flooded with *good* news—right? Whereas if an optimist is wrong it isn't going to end well. I changed from my natural outlook and started to think positively.

Press '1' For Lost Luggage

I had a phone number to call.

The chap at Heathrow sounded confident and seemed to know what he was talking about.

So, let's try to look on the bright side.

It had now been six hours since I had left the lost luggage desk, so it was time for a check in. I settled in my parents' front room, picked up the phone and dialled the number to start the seemingly eternal round of options to get to the right department, based on airline, departure airport and destination. After around five minutes of digital interrogation into where I wanted my call to be directed, I heard a ringing tone, signalling the first sign of hope that I would be able to speak to someone… then I heard a recorded message telling me, "There is currently a large volume of calls, and someone would be with me 'shortly'."

And then it started: the crappy soundtrack of shit 1980s soft rock music.

My mum walked into the room and asked me what was happening.

I was on hold.

"Oh dear," she said and walked back into the kitchen shaking her head.

"He's on hold," I heard her tell my dad.

"There're bloody hopeless," he replied.

After I had spent about ten minutes sitting on the sofa looking out the window while listening to a mixture of Wham! Abba and Boney M, my mum walked back in and asked me what was happening.

I was still on hold.

"Oh dear," she said and walked back into the kitchen shaking her head.

"He's still on hold," she told my dad.

"There're bloody hopeless," he replied.

After another ten minutes she was back.

"Are you still on hold?" she asked.

"Yes."

"Oh dear. He's still on hold Roy," she shouted through to the kitchen.

"They're bloody hopeless," came the loud response.

"Your dad's getting hungry, is it okay if I get on with dinner?" she asked.

"Yes, of course," I said. "I can bring the phone with me to the table."

"Okay then." And off she went with a shake of the head.

"He's still on hold," I heard as she got to the kitchen.

"Bloody hopeless."

Dinner was a tense affair.

It was like someone had died.

The phone handset was next to me on "speaker" setting, but at least it was a first in that household that our dinner background music was provided by Wham!, Abba and Boney M, which made a change to have shit 1980s soft rock instead of the shit classical dross churned out by Classic FM (if only they would play a few Mahler symphonies, or Bruckner, maybe try a bit of Richard Strauss, or excerpts from Gotterdammerung).

With dinner done it was time to take the "optimism" down to new depths.

My dad asked me what time the place I was calling closed?

Didn't have a clue.

My mum suggested it was time to call it a day and try again tomorrow, then asked me if I knew anyone in Canada who worked for Air Canada, and would they be able to help?

No, and if I did it would be highly unlikely they would.

My dad told me to go and sit on the sofa while he and my mum cleared up the dishes.

I did as they requested. They cleaned while emitting a lot of sighing and tutting.

"Brown girl in the ring, la di da di dah..." you know the treatment/punishment is working when you start to sing along.

My mum walked in.

"Still on hold?

"Yes."

"Oh dear. What are you going to do?"

"I haven't really got any options, have I?"

"I don't suppose so," she said as she departed for the kitchen again.

"He's still on hold, Roy".

"Bloody hopeless."

And then, just as George Michael started what must have been the fiftieth rendition of "Wake me up before you go go…." the music changed to a ringing tone, shortly followed by a live human voice.

"Hello, how can I help you?"

"Oh hello, I flew into Heathrow this morning from Toronto and my bag was lost on the way. I'm following up…"

"Are you talking to someone?" I heard my mum ask as she walked into the room again.

"Yes."

"What are they saying?"

"Shush, I can't hear them."

"He's talking to someone," she shouted to my dad.

"About bloody time."

"I'm sorry," I said to the lady on the phone. "I'm following up on my lost bag from my flight from Toronto this morning. Could you give me an update please?"

"I can't do that," she said, "but you can go to our website, it's at…" After which she gave me a URL, repeated it so I could write it down, and hung up.

Oh, happy days.

So, it was to my laptop I went, which had thankfully been in my carry-on bag, and on to the website I'd been given.

I found the relevant page, entered my details and the reference number from the form I was given at Heathrow, clicked "search," and eureka! There was my bag—still in Toronto.

"How are you getting on?" asked my mum.

"Well, it looks like I've found my bag."

"Oh good, where is it?"

"Still in Toronto."

"Oh no. His bag's still in Toronto, Roy."

"Bloody hopeless."

More research told me the bag was due to be put on the overnight flight to Heathrow and would be in London the following morning. The green shoots of hope had raised their heads above the ground, so it was off for a jetlag-affected sleep while my mum got to work on washing the only clothes I had with me so they would be ready for the morning.

The next day the sun rose over the beautiful Derbyshire countryside, my mum had the bacon and eggs on the go and my laptop was quickly opened in order to get a bag status update.

Yes, it was on the overnight flight and would arrive at Heathrow at 8:30 a.m.

The drive was around three hours, so the worst-case scenario suggested it would be with me by late afternoon, giving me plenty of time to unpack and get things ironed and ready for my meeting the next day.

Mother's Tramp

Morning turned to afternoon and no sign of the bag.

Now, my parents lived in a fairly remote part of a very small village in the Derbyshire Peak District and if you didn't know how to navigate the narrow lanes and side streets, you'd drive around for hours trying to find their house.

"They'll never find us here, no one ever does," said my dad which, while *sounding* pessimistic was actually very accurate, though not encouraging.

"You could call and tell them how to find us," added mum.

It is often better to just comply with an idea than argue. I went to the website, found a phone number and dialled. At least the music had graduated from shit 1980s soft rock to shit 1990s soft rock.

"He's on hold again," my mum told my dad as she returned to the kitchen.

"I bet he is," came the response.

In fairness, it only took around thirty-five minutes for someone to speak on the other end, and once my details were received and my intent to explain directions presented, I was advised to call back on Thursday with the information.

Thursday?

THURSDAY??

But today's Tuesday.

Apparently, they only dispatched bags by courier on Mondays and Thursdays, but at least I would have it by the weekend.

It was now around 6:00 p.m.—dinner time for my dad—so eat we did and started also to formulate a clothing plan for the next day.

"You can't wear those clothes you arrived in to that meeting," said my mum, "they are awful."

"They are actually very comfortable," I replied.

"You look terrible in them. I'm really surprised at you for wearing them, you look like a tramp."

"They are great for travelling."

"Well, you can't wear them tomorrow. I mean, who wears sweatpants and a rugby shirt to a business meeting?"

"You know what, mum, we should really get you on Mastermind (a very intellectual BBC Quiz Show). Next contestant please. Name? Wendy Weston. Specialist Subject? The Bleeding Obvious. I'm not going to wear these clothes tomorrow."

"What are you going to wear then?"

"I don't know yet."

"You could try one of your dad's suits."

My dad was 5'8" tall and weighed around 160 pounds.

I was 6'00" tall and weighed nearly 200 pounds.

"My suits won't fit him," said my dad.

"You don't know that," said mum.

"Of course they won't, look at him and look at me."

"Well, what are you going to do then?"

"My meeting is at 2:00 p.m. It's the other side of Manchester, which is about a ninety-minute drive, so I can go early and call in at the Trafford Centre (a large shopping mall in Manchester on the way to my appointment) and get something."

"You mean buy new clothes?"

"Well what else am I going to do?"

"There might be someone round here can lend you something," she countered.

The village of Bradwell in Derbyshire is inhabited by a general mixture of old people and farmers. I didn't know that many people but couldn't imagine any of the ones I did know possessing the sort of clothes I would require.

"I'm not knocking on doors begging for clothes," I said.

"You wouldn't be begging; you'd be returning them. I can wash everything and take them back."

"You can't wash a suit."

"Well, I can get a suit dry-cleaned if it needs it, but I can wash your shirt."

"I'm not doing that; I'll try the shops at the Trafford Centre."

"Do you want your dad to come with you?" my mum queried.

"Why?"

"To help you."

"To help me with what?"

"To make sure you get a proper suit and everything."

I was forty-five years old at the time.

"I think I'll be fine thanks."

"He doesn't mind, do you, Roy?"

"No, I can come with you."

"It's fine, really, plus I will be going straight to the meeting after that."

"You can't go straight to the meeting!" exclaimed my mum.

"Why not?" I asked.

"The suit will need pressing and everything, and the shirt—it will have been in a packet."

"I'll just keep my jacket on. Anyway, I'm not driving to Manchester to buy clothes, to come back here, iron them, then drive all the way back to other side of Manchester. It will be fine."

"Oh dear," said my mum while rolling her eyes and shaking her head.

And so it was decided. Well, my mum clearly wasn't very happy, but at least I now had a plan.

Sick Day

Wednesday arrived, and notwithstanding the suit drama, the contents of my suitcase I was missing the most were my running shoes, shirts and shorts. I love to run whenever I travel, and the Derbyshire Peak District has some of the most beautiful scenery, trails and paths to be found anywhere, so I was missing my regular early morning outings. I could have worn my "tramp clothes" but then I would have had nothing to wear for the rest of the day while my mum washed them (again).

After another hearty breakfast for my mum's "growing lad," I was off in search of clothing redemption and the joys of the Trafford Centre. There were a number of stores that carried suits, but as I have never really been at the cutting edge of fashion (or anything else for that matter), I settled for Marks and Spencer. They were able to provide me with a dark grey suit, two shirts (keep reading, you'll soon see why), black socks (two pairs) a couple of ties, and the most "sensible" pair of black shoes I have ever owned. I have always wondered about "sensible" shoes. Every time there was a school trip, the instructions on the letter sent home were for us all to wear "sensible" shoes. When I played in youth orchestras and bands, we were told the concert dress should include "sensible" shoes. Church Parade in the Scouts required our best uniforms and "sensible" shoes.

Did "sensible" mean the shoes had to be of a certain maturity level—that they wouldn't mess around and get into trouble? Or was it an-IQ based requirement—the shoes had to have a score of at least 100 to justify their "sensible" status?

But my visit to the Marks and Spencer gentlemen's footwear department that morning clarified my decades-long quest for the truth. "Sensible" really meant "boring" or "ugly" or "middle-aged" (as applied to the wearer, not the shoes, which were obviously very young). Once tried on and paid for, I returned to the changing room to put on the suit, shirt (one), tie (one), socks (one pair) and the sensible shoes. Although slightly creased, I was confident I could "wing it" without the lady I was meeting with thinking 'he just bought that'.

I got some lunch (careful not to spill anything and ruin my new look) and headed off to said meeting. On arrival, I parked, entered the offices and walked up to the reception desk where a rather attractive young lady greeted me with one of those "my, don't you look smart today?" looks and asked how she could help. The most truthful answer I could have given here would have been "find out where my bloody bag is," but that wouldn't have solved anything.

"I'm here to see Iris Wilkins," I said.

"I'm sorry," she replied, "Iris is sick today and won't be in."

"My, don't you look smart?" said my mum as I walked in through the door. "How was your meeting?"

"The woman I was meeting was off sick."

"Oh no, couldn't she have called you?"

"Apparently, they tried, but as it was an international call to my cell phone, they couldn't get through. They sent an email this morning, but I couldn't get a signal at the Trafford Centre so didn't see it until it was too late."

"Bloody hopeless," said my dad.

From there I was due to travel on the Friday to Portsmouth for a military reunion dinner on Saturday and a Memorial Church service on the Sunday. I was getting the feeling I might never be reunited with my bag, hence the purchase of additional shirts, ties and socks. I also bought some casual clothes to keep me covered, as well. I followed up to pass on directions to the courier on Thursday only to be told my bag was listed to leave on Friday.

This was actually good news as directions to my Portsmouth hotel were much simpler than those to my parents' house, and so with a "you look a lot smarter leaving than you did when you arrived," from my mum, I headed south, confident that my arrival in Portsmouth would herald a reunion with my bag, and running gear, meaning I could indulge in another of my favourite running routes along Southsea sea front.

Alas, the bag wasn't in Portsmouth on Friday. Neither did it arrive on Saturday, and the courier office was closed until Monday morning—the day I was due to fly back to Canada. This also meant I was fined a bottle of port at the reunion for not wearing my Regimental tie (I think the Marks and Spencer tie department is missing a trick there).

I was up early on Monday morning. I had a 2:00 p.m. flight from Heathrow to Toronto, but first I called the courier office as soon as it was open at 8:00 a.m. to discover my bag was still there.

"Where are you located?" I asked.

"We are about thirty miles north of Heathrow," the lady on the other end of the line said. "Your bag is first in line for dispatch this morning. It's going to Derbyshire—correct?"

"DO NOT SEND IT ANYWHERE," I very nearly screamed into the phone. "I will collect it from you this morning, I'll be there in a couple of hours."

"We don't allow people to collect bags from us," the woman on the other end replied.

I wasn't having any of this and told her how my week had gone. She succumbed but told me to call her from the car park when I arrived, and she would bring it out as her boss would be angry if she allowed me to come in and collect it.

I didn't call. I wanted to take it up with the boss, so I walked into her office.

He was off sick, but there was my bag, all on its lonesome.

Once we had gone through something of an emotional reunion (the bag and me, not the lady in the office), I headed off to Heathrow, returned my car and went to the Air Canada desk to check in and drop my bag for its return journey.

Of course, there were no glitches in the system on the way back, and my bag was one of the first on the carousel—but this time it didn't really matter too much.

And so began a litany of lost luggage "adventures."

A year later, one of my business trips took me to San Francisco for a few days while my bag stayed in Toronto. Air Canada did actually succeed in getting it to me within twenty-four hours, but I had learned to carry toiletries and some basic clothes in my carry-on bag.

In 2013 my wife (at the time) and I were due to fly to Vancouver Island to visit her sister. She had planned the tickets which routed us through Vancouver where we would pick up a car and get the ferry to Nanaimo, close to where the sister and her family lived. As we checked the bags, we noticed the Air Canada staff member put a yellow tag on each bag.

"What are they for?" I asked.

"Well, as you (the "you" being my wife at the time) used an online agency to book your tickets rather than the Air Canada site, you don't actually have seats on this flight until everyone else has checked in," she said with something of a smirk.

"What?!"

She repeated her answer, with the hint of additional smirk.

"We don't have seats?"

"No. Look at your boarding passes—you are on "Standby." You can go to the gate and wait there. One of you may get on the aircraft, but I doubt both of you will. This is a busy flight."

We got to the gate to be told that everyone had checked in and we were not going anywhere. There was another flight to Vancouver in six hours and we were booked on that one. But all was not lost, and my wife, feeling somewhat guilty for the booking infraction, took up the reins.

A week or so earlier she had had an accident in the gym and broken her wrist. It had been set and was in a cast and she lifted her arm to show the attendant. She stated that we were going to visit her sister with a broken wrist (her wrist of course, not her sister's). Now, while this may not have had a lot of sway with me, it worked, because the very helpful lady took pity on us and managed to get us seats on a different flight directly to Victoria, which is on Vancouver Island, rather than the City of Vancouver, and not just regular seats, but in Business Class. This immediately cheered us up, and my only query was, "what would happen to our luggage?"

"Don't worry," she said, "they will be put on this aircraft."

We had a couple of hours to wait, during which I managed to change the rental car reservation and cancel the ferry; then we were boarding. Sitting in very comfortable seats and sipping champagne, we were soon airborne when I was hit with a dose of realism.

"This is very nice," I said, "but I have absolutely no faith that our bags are on this aircraft."

"The eternal optimist strikes again," said the wife.

"Well, do *you* have faith they are with us?"

"I will remain confident they are," she said.

We were on the last flight into Victoria that evening, where the airport is a rather small and intimate affair. There were only a few carousels, and it didn't take long for the bags to start appearing. One by one owners claimed their belongings and headed out to wherever they were going until, with no bags left, the carousel ground to a halt. Staring in despair at the outcome of a long day of travel, I could at least revel in the fact my prediction had been proven right.

"YES!' I shouted, "SEE, I WAS RIGHT—our bags weren't the plane! HA!"

The win came with a price of course, and it was off to Baggage Services, where the attendant was winding everything down for the night as the airport was about to close.

"Guess what?" we asked him.

"No bags?"

"Correct."

He did what they all do and took down our details. His research told him they were still in Toronto and due to be on the next flight to... Vancouver.

"Why Vancouver if you are here in Victoria?"

I explained the change in flights etc. and he made appropriate changes to the notes. In this case, the bags did arrive the next day and were couriered to the Airbnb we were staying at in Nanaimo, but because we were out when they arrived, the driver decided it was okay to leave them at the bottom of the driveway... in the rain.

If It Works for George

There was also an occasion when my bag went to a country on its own without me.

In 2017 I was working with some clients in Europe and the Middle East. My bag and I successfully travelled to Frankfurt, Germany, and once my work was done, I was booked on a Lufthansa flight to Jeddah, Saudi Arabia. My bag made it to Jeddah, but the trouble was, the aircraft was then heading on to Addis Ababa in Ethiopia, which is where my bag ended up as the ground crew in Jeddah failed to remove it from the aircraft. Once again, I had to deal with a new Baggage Services process and although they assured me there was a return flight back along the same route in the morning, I had little faith I would see my bag in the immediate future. And so, once I had checked in at my hotel, it was off to explore the clothing options of Jeddah, and, to my surprise, found another Marks and Spencer (who'd have thought?!). But in this case, I had to guess what underwear I was buying as the local religious laws required that photographs on packaging of men's underwear in Marks and Spencer had to be covered up with black tape.

I was there for five days (Jeddah, not Marks and Spencer), and despite daily phone calls to the airport, there was no sign of my bag. My return journey to Canada was via the UK, during which I would spend a few days with my parents (enduring the latest inquest into my lost luggage). By now I had given up on Jeddah airport services and had taken things up with Lufthansa, which led to the discovery of an interesting fact: the customer services department for lost luggage of passengers who live in Canada is based in the Philippines and is only open during Philippine working hours. This meant staying up late or getting up ridiculously early, to be put on hold for very long periods of time (listening to some shit Philippine soft rock), only to discover they had absolutely no idea where my bag was.

I had all but given up hope when, after about six weeks, I was on a call with the client I had been working with in Jeddah who asked me if I ever got my bag back.

Nope.

He said he would go out to the airport to see if he could track it down, and then, a few hours later, sent me a photo of a bag asking if this was it?

It was!

Apparently, it had arrived in Saudi the morning after I had, but the passenger services staff weren't allowed to make international phone calls (something to do with national security) so couldn't call my Canadian cell phone number to tell me. Neither could they enter my details into their system, so when I called each day, no one knew who I was. Thanks to my Saudi contact, the bag was recovered and dispatched back to Canada.

This was pretty much the final straw, but coincided with me watching a film called *Up in the Air* featuring George Clooney playing the part of a business executive who spends around 90% of his life travelling around the country. His travel modus operandi is to *only* take carry-on luggage, and that is where my life was transformed. Rather than take enough clothes to last me for the duration of my trip, I now take two of everything and a small bag of laundry powder so I can handwash everything each night. Carry-on only probably saves me several days' worth of time every year. It is easy to check in, you know your bag is with you at all times, and there is no need to wait for your luggage at the arrival airport.

But there have still been times when I do have to check luggage, notably when flying to triathlon races and in 2022, I entered an Ironman in the UK. Air Canada has now introduced an app where you can track your luggage and they indeed send you a notification when your bag has been loaded onto the aircraft. In this case I had two checked bags: my bike, and a bag with my wetsuit and cycling equipment (shoes helmet etc.), and as we were just pushing back from the gate, I got a message that while my bike was onboard, my equipment bag wasn't. I would be in the UK for about a week before the race, so didn't panic too much, but when I headed to the Baggage Services desk at Heathrow Airport to report the loss and hand over my parents' address where I was staying, apart from a feeling of déjà vu, their systems seemed a lot more modern. There were automated screens to fill in the relevant details, after which I received an email telling me I was in the system and I could use it to track my bag—which, they reliably informed me, was still safely in Toronto.

And so, I headed back out into the baggage reclaim area and the various revolving carousels towards the exit, and passed the Toronto one and, hold on… isn't that my bag?

YES!

What goes around comes around (pun intended), and from losing a bag to finding it was something of a minor miracle, even though Air Canada never did follow up to see if I had recovered it.

I have always enjoyed travel, but the baggage piece can be stressful; I now generally only take carry-on but, when I can't, those lost-bag hills can be tough ones to run up.

CHAPTER 3

A Hill Called Packaging

*M*any years ago, I played in a game of rugby between my club, Deal Wanderers, and a local Kent league rival, Snowden Colliery. As with most local rivalries, it was an acrimonious affair with many players having quite a few scores to settle. However, as this was my Deal/Snowden debut, I assumed my card wasn't in anyway "marked" and as the team's Fly Half[3] I thought I would be left in peace to ply my trade for the afternoon.

Not so.

After around fifteen minutes we won a lineout[4], and the ball found its way to our scrum half[5] who then dispatched it swiftly on to me. As we had a deep line and quick possession, I moved the ball on to our inside centre and headed behind our attacking line to see where I might take a supporting pass and break through Snowden's defensive line. In rugby, there is a fairly important law: you cannot

---

[3] In rugby a fly half is a key playmaker typically positioned behind the bigger, heavier forward players. For North American readers, it's similar in some senses to a quarterback, except they have to run, tackle and kick, and they stay on the field for the entire game—so nothing like a quarterback really.

[4] Essentially an opportunity to restart play.

[5] The scrum half is a key player in rugby and, in particular, they get the game rolling again after a lineout.

tackle someone who is not in possession of the ball. At least, you are not *supposed to*. However, in this instance the "laws" were pretty much secondary to the general intent—which was to smash the other team up as much as possible. And so, around twenty seconds after passing the ball—and well out of the referee's line of sight—I took a blow to the side of my head that felt like I'd missed the level crossing gates and red flashing lights and run straight into the path of a fifty-car freight train.

I hit the ground like the proverbial sack of shit with bells ringing in my head and stars dancing across my vision. But that wasn't the end of it. As I rolled over onto my hands and knees, a very large boot, with long metal studs, was stamped down onto my left hand with such force that within a matter of a minute, the back of it had swollen so much it looked like I had stuffed a cricket ball under the skin. The pain was excruciating, and my game, for that afternoon, was over. I was dispatched to hospital and the x-ray department, which clearly identified a broken metacarpal and trapezoid. The injury would require a cast, but not until the swelling had receded to the point my hand at least *looked* normal.

I was sent home in a sling, and with a bottle of prescription painkillers.

At the time, I shared a house with two other guys, both of whom were also part of the rugby club, and as this was, by now, Saturday evening, they were, as you might expect, "out on the piss," and although not wanting to miss out on any fun, I took the mature—and very unusual for me at that time in my life—decision, to stay home.

Pain.

It's an interesting phenomenon. I suppose it is nature's way of telling you something—like stop playing rugby? Yeah right! Or better still, "don't do that with your hand—it's broken." But while that message is clear, have you ever tried to *not* do anything with your hand? Every movement, every little nudge, seemingly every breath sent a shock wave of agony throughout my whole body. But I had prescription painkillers, didn't I? Time to get all drugged up then, right?

Wrong.

Child proof container.

I can see the reasoning behind their existence, I mean, we don't want kids getting addicted to opioids and all that, but at the same time, if they want to go down the addiction pathway to self-destruction, there are plenty of opportunities other than through prescription drugs. But the "powers that be" had decided that those little tablets of agony relief were not going to be made available without a fight.

At this point, allow me to ask you to consider a simple question:

Have you ever struggled to open a child proof pill bottle and *not* had some issues? You know the type: you have to hold the bottle with one hand and either push down the top while turning or align two microscopically small plastic arrows before finding an 18-inch chisel to prise the top off or squeeze the bottle top together with the same amount of force it would take to split an atom.

And, of course, the traditional technique you might employ would require the use of *two* hands.

But picture the scene that evening. One hand by now the size of a small African country. An empty house. A full bottle of painkillers. And a lot of agony with no way of opening said bottle.

Packaging.

Sponges Have Feelings Too You Know

Plastic is a thought-provoking material. There are lots of downsides in that it doesn't go away easily, but it is also really useful. I'd never thought about some of its more interesting uses, but when a plastic manufacturing company called Ineos, which I had never heard of, took over the team sponsorship—and effectively the ownership—

of the World Pro Tour Cycling Team previously known as Team Sky, in 2019, their team principal, Dave Brailsford (of British Olympic Cycling fame) suddenly got all "pro-plastic."

You may expect this from a good "team player" (he wasn't going to turn all Greta Thunberg on us if he wanted to keep his job, was he?). But as Ineos is one of the largest producers of plastic on the planet, he was quickly briefed.

His message related to how beneficial plastic was to the world.

He made some good points. Look at the plastic on a modern car or aeroplane, making them lighter, more fuel efficient and consequently better for the environment (got you there, Greta). Next time you are in a hospital operating theatre (I've been in a few), look around and imagine what it would look like without any plastic. But… when you flip the page to the negatives, you don't have to look far to start having issues with the amount of stuff they use to wrap up the smallest item.

I recently went to my local grocery store to get my usual food supplies as well as some dish washing sponges—you know the type, yellow sponge with a green "scrubby" bit on the top. I selected a packet of forty to keep me going (no electrical dishwashers in my house, Greta), which were, understandably, contained in a plastic packet. But when I got home and opened them up, I discovered they were all also individually wrapped in plastic.

Why?

I mean, if it was food and they wanted to separate the items, then I might get it, but *dishwashing sponges*? Were they worried they might not get along and wanted to keep them apart, like my teacher used to do on school trips with the annoying kids?

Were they worried the green bits might scratch the yellow bits of another sponge and cause some offence? It was pure madness that so much plastic had been allocated to such a ridiculous product.

Then there was the day plastic nearly got me arrested.

The story starts one Saturday afternoon in February during the late 1990s.

I was sitting on my sofa at home watching some international rugby, which required flicking between two channels as my team, England—who I desperately wanted to win—were playing France, and on another channel, Wales—who I desperately wanted to lose—were playing Scotland. Little did I know that I was about to endure what was probably one of the most devastating experiences of my life, something that has scarred my mind ever since, something which even to this day causes me to wake in the middle of the night in a cold sweat and a blood-curdling scream of despair.

My TV remote stopped working.

This meant, of course, that to change channels, I had to get up off the sofa, walk across the room, press a button on the TV, and walk back to the sofa, only to discover that Wales had just scored another try, and it was better to go back to the England game.

Up and down, up and down. The afternoon was turning into the ultimate nightmare.

But, as halftime approached, my strategic plan to recover the situation was forming: new batteries. A long blast from the referee's whistle meant that while the players went off for their halftime oranges (and a good bollocking in England's case), I moved swiftly into my kitchen and the drawer containing my battery supply. The back came off the remote, the two old doubles As were removed and of course I then had to attack the new battery package with a pair of scissors to get through the customary plastic—they could just as easily be stored and transported in cardboard—in order to remove two fresh batteries and insert them into the remote.

With the back snapped smartly into place, it was back to the sofa and a return to life making a little more sense again. As the England team were by now jogging out onto the field, I decided to catch up on the Wales game in the hope there had been a turnaround.

I pointed the remote at the TV and clicked. And clicked. And clicked again.

Nothing.

The red transmit light on the remote was working (something I should have checked before replacing the batteries), but still I was watching the English lining up opposite the French to resume the latest version of Waterloo.

Click. Click (what's that definition of insanity?) and click again. Still nothing.

I resorted to sticking with England for another twenty minutes or so before getting up and checking in on Wales.

Despair, not only from the Wales game, but the fact my whole televisual experience was ruined.

But, once the rugby was over, my strategic juices were flowing and, knowing there is always a solution (I just had to find it), I went through the options.

The remote was clearly powered up as the light kept coming on. But maybe it wasn't able to transmit a signal. Was the little glass bubble at the front dirty? I got out my glass cleaner fluid and cloth (both wrapped in plastic) and gave it a squirt and a wipe. The TV was now showing the English football league scores, and my new attempt to switch channels resulted in… nothing.

And so, I resorted to what any self-respecting bloke would do— took the back off the remote and looked inside.

There was what looked like a plastic board with coloured wires and shiny metal things stuck to it. There was a small cylindrical shape with a wire coming out leading into a silvery spot that looked like solder. I had no idea what I was supposed to be looking for—maybe I was living in the false hope that I would see something really obvious, like the end of a redundant wire and some form of receptacle just waiting to be reunited—so I cast an eye over the whole scene, blew on it (stop the eye-rolling at the back there, there could easily have been some dust clogging things up), and replaced the back.

By now, the BBC had moved on to the news and, after a gentle intake of breath and an outpouring of hope, I pointed and clicked.

And clicked. And clicked.

Nothing.

In yet more despair, I slumped onto the sofa.

During my younger adult days, I had lived in a house that can best be described as "suitable accommodation for three beer-drinking-rugby-playing-Royal-Marines-musicians," and although we had a very large TV, it was also very old and built around the time remote controls were barely a twinkle in some entertainment equipment designer's eye. We changed channels by way of four large buttons just below the screen—none of your thousands of digital options then—and in order to switch from *Coronation Street* to *Top of the Pops*, we used an old snooker cue… not forgetting to chalk the tip, of course, in order to achieve maximum purchase and control on the button.

But those days were gone.

But now my longest piece of sporting apparatus was a golf club, and in particular, my driver, but of course this wasn't anywhere close to the length of a snooker cue and, anyway, the channel buttons were so small you could hardly see them even from three feet away. Alas, a dark and gloomy cloud settled over my home, and I had to resort to a weekend of frustrating TV watching, which, if nothing else, made me truly appreciate the genius who designed the remote control in the first place.

Monday arrived. A new week meant a fresh opportunity to tackle any new challenges that would head my way. But no matter my professional responsibilities, my principal aim was to solve my TV-watching challenges, and having done pretty much all I could with the battery replenishment strategy, had concluded that my handheld piece of joy was faulty and beyond salvage. I was going to have to purchase a complete new remote.

Dave: Where Have You Been All My Life?

So, on my way home from work, I called in at my local electrical appliance store. On entering, I quickly found the appropriate aisle and began assessing the various options, one of which was an identical replica of my current model. But the packaging it was contained in made me start to believe it was as sensitive as a nuclear warhead. And, of course, the packaging wasn't made of paper or cardboard. Nor was it a light wrapping of thin plastic, or something one could easily open to remove the item inside and, if required, replace it, and then snap the packaging shut again. No, the packaging looked like it had been welded shut, as the two sides of plastic were surrounded by a secure crimp-like seal that I knew was going to require very strong scissors to open.

Or even a pair of garden shears.

Or a circular saw.

Maybe bolt croppers, a large guillotine or possibly a machete.

But what bothered me about the packaging (apart from the usual over-abundance of plastic) was the fact that to open it would result in catastrophically fatal damage to the extent it could not be re-sealed and returned should it not, indeed, be the remote at fault.

I needed some professional advice, so headed off to secure the help of a sales assistant.

What seemed like four days later, I finally found one that wasn't "helping with another customer," didn't "work in that particular department," or was busy "replenishing the video games shelves."

My particular favourite was the woman working on the "Customer Service" desk: she watched me approach until I was three paces away, at which point she picked up the phone and started dialing, while looking at me with a smirk the like of which would curdle milk.

The sales assistant whose services I did indeed manage to engage was just heading to lunch, so I had to move fast.

"I have a very quick and simple question I hope you can answer regarding this remote control."

"What? I'm in a hurry," she said.

"I have the exact same model at home that is not working—well, I am not able to change channels using the remote, which means I have to get up and walk across the room every time I want to switch from *Coronation Street* to *Top of the Pops*."

"That must be very annoying," she said, with just a hint of sarcasm.

"You have no idea," I replied.

"No, I wouldn't," she said, "I don't watch Coronation Street."

"Really? I thought *everyone* watched *Coronation Street*."

"Not me, I'm an *Eastenders* fan."

"That just seems like too much mental anguish to me."

"No. I love it."

"Anyway," I continued, "my question is: as you can see, this remote is securely packaged in a way that means it would require cutting open with at least some scissors." I didn't add the other options mentioned above—I like to feel I am above fighting sarcasm with sarcasm.

"Yes, it is," she replied.

"So, what if I get it home, put batteries in and point it at the TV and it still doesn't work?"

"Meaning, of course, you would have to keep getting up and walking across the room," she replied, this time a with definite tone of sarcasm.

"Correct. Anyway, if indeed it *isn't* the remote that is faulty, am I able to return it for a refund if the packing is damaged?"

"Yes."

"Really?"

"Yes."

"Are you sure?"

"Yes—as long as you have a receipt, you can return it."

"Even if I have cut open the packaging?"

"Yes."

"Okay, thank you."

"You are welcome—may I go to lunch now?" she asked, with a final wedge of pure sarcasm.

I headed to the checkout to pay for my new remote, handed over what felt like a financial commitment in excess of what I had originally paid for the complete TV itself only four years previously, and drove home to, hopefully, restore my TV-watching pleasure to its former glory.

On arrival in my kitchen, I dug around in my cutlery draw to find my finest Sheffield Steel scissors and introduced them to the impending challenge.

But not even the finest blades Yorkshire can offer were a match for this task. They barely made a mark on what seemed like a three-inch-thick protective screen and trying to force the blades closed on such depth nearly dislocated my thumb.

Off to my tool kit and my rather aged Stanley knife, but while this enabled me to cut through the plastic, it did not allow me to fully separate the two sides as the crimped edge was just too tough. While I had made a reasonably wide hole, I could not actually break the plastic open, meaning I had to get some fingers inside, and try to force the remote back through the gap while keeping the sides apart. This resulted in such force on my knuckles, it drew blood through the sharpness of the edge.

But, my fortitude, determination and cheerfulness of character shone through, and I was able to extricate the object of my intent. The battery compartment was opened, new batteries installed, and, as the TV was on at the time, the ultimate channel switch test awaited.

I settled on the sofa, took a deep breath… pointed… and clicked.

Nothing.

I clicked again.

Nothing.

"Bugger," said I. I actually said several words that were a lot stronger, but I'm never quite sure who reads my stuff, so you'll have to imagine that part.

The situation was now getting very serious.

The little red light on the new remote was working, which suggested the remote was, as per the old one, transmitting a signal, but clearly the TV was not receiving. This would require further investigation, but right now my aim was to return the new remote and claim my refund.

On my return home the following day, I called in at the store again.

This time I went straight to the customer service counter, where I caught the woman from the previous day off guard, not allowing her the opportunity to pick up the phone to make another fake call.

Her name badge advised me she was known as Doreen.

"Yes?" she said. I assumed it was a question and that asking me how she might be able to help was just too much work.

"I'd like to return this please," I replied, while placing the receipt and the remote—which was now back inside the badly damaged packaging—on the desk.

"Why, what's wrong with it?" she asked.

"I bought it as I thought my old remote was broken, but when I got it home, I found it isn't the remote as this one doesn't work either. It must be the TV, so consequently, I would like to return it please."

"You can't return this."

"Why not?"

"You've opened it."

"Well of course I've opened it, how else was I supposed to try it to see if it was the remote or the TV?"

"But you've damaged the packaging."

"It's not possible to open the packaging without damaging it—obviously. I mean look at it. How was I supposed to open it without cutting it open?" I asked.

"You can't return an item if the packaging is damaged."

"Once again, how was I supposed to know if it was indeed the remote that wasn't working without trying it and how could I try it without taking it out of the packaging and how was I supposed to open the packaging without damaging it?"

"That's not my problem."

"What do you mean by that?"

"It's not our policy to accept returns if the packaging has been damaged—so it's not my problem."

"Ah, but a member of your staff assured me yesterday that if it wasn't the remote, as long as I had the receipt, I could return it."

"No, they didn't."

"Yes, they did."

"None of our staff would say that because they all know our policy."

"Well, that's why I checked with her before I bought it."

"I doubt you did."

This was getting very annoying now.

"Look, I know what I was told, and if I had been told what you are telling me now, I wouldn't have bought the bloody thing in the first place."

"Please stop using offensive language, or I will have to ask you to leave the store."

"Please try to understand my perspective on this. I specifically asked about your returns policy for this reason, and I am very annoyed that what I was told is not being honoured."

"Well, whatever, we are not going to give you a refund."

"Okay, enough. I'd like to speak to your manager please."

"He'll only give you the same answer."

"Well, I'd like to hear it directly from him. Is he around?"

At this point she picked up the phone handset, pressed a button and made a public announcement asking the store manager to come to customer service.

Which is when I met Dave.

"What's your problem?" he asked.

Note that, once again, it was *my* problem. Not *the* problem. Not *the store's* problem, but all *mine*.

I repeated what I had said to Doreen.

"We can't give you a refund," replied Dave.

"Can't or won't?" I asked.

"It's not our policy to give refunds if you've damaged the packaging."

"Yes, I was just made aware of that, which, as I have just tried to explain, is why I asked one of your staff about it yesterday."

"I bet you didn't."

"You can bet I did mate," I said, although it was unlikely Dave and I were ever going to meet up for a beer and a good catch-up anytime soon.

"Which member of our staff?"

"She wasn't wearing a name badge, but it was a middle-aged lady with blond hair. She was just going to lunch when I was here," I said before looking around the store to see if she was there. She wasn't, but I thought at least they would know who I was talking about.

"I don't know who you mean," said Dave.

"You must do—you're the manager, aren't you?"

"Of course, I am—but I don't know who you mean?"

"She likes watching Eastenders, that must narrow it down a bit."

"So?"

"So, I know I was speaking with a woman on your staff to the point I know what she likes to watch on TV, and if I can remember that, then I can remember what she told me about returning this remote."

"Look mate, we can't give you a refund if you have damaged the packaging because we can't sell it again like this can we?"

"But that really isn't my problem if that was what I was told though is it? Surely you can return it to the manufacturer?"

"I can only return it to the manufacturer if it doesn't work."

This was an opening that both of us could now leverage towards a solution. Come on Dave, work with me here.

"Okay," I said. "It doesn't work."

"What do you mean?" asked Dave. He wasn't going for it.

"I mean I'm telling you I took it home, opened it up, tried it and... found it doesn't work. So, you can return it to whomever, and I can have my refund and we're all happy."

"But it does work."

"How do you know? You haven't tried it."

"I bet if I tried it on one of our TVs it would work."

"But you would have to cut the packaging open first wouldn't you, just to find out?'

"No, I wouldn't. It's already open."

"See my point?"

"What point?" ·

"THE WHOLE POINT OF MY ISSUE HERE." This particular hill was getting very steep now.

"Look, we are not going to give you a refund because you have damaged the packaging, so I'm going to ask you to leave the store."

Now, I have always considered myself to be a reasonable man and am usually willing to make a compromise for the benefit of others, so I thought I would put an alternative proposition on the table.

"I'll tell you what Dave, I do a lot of shopping here, so I would accept a store credit. How about that?"

"Nope."

"Why not?"

"Because, once again, we cannot resell this item as the packaging is damaged—and that is the last time I am going to tell you that."

With that I picked up the remote and my receipt, glared at Dave, turned around and walked out onto the street.

Over Here Greta

Now, everyone has a breaking point, and Dave had just taken me to mine. I stopped outside the door, took stock of my situation and decided that NO, this is wrong, and I am not going to accept it.

So, I turned around and went back into the store and up to the customer service desk once again, whereupon Doreen saw me and started shrieking at the top her voice.

"DAVE, DAVE, he's back, he's back—DAVE, DAVE."

Dave came rushing back, but I was ready with the opening words of the fresh encounter.

"Look this is totally ridiculous. I bought this remote in good faith as I was told I could return it, but you are not willing to support the information I was given by a member of your staff. This is simply not acceptable—I WANT MY MONEY BACK!"

The last five words were shouted very loudly to the point everyone in the store heard them.

Dave was now looking angry.

"Look mate, I have told you what our policy is, there is NO WAY you are getting your money back—now leave my store or I will call the police."

"Go ahead," I said, and sat down on the floor.

Now, while Greta may have been proud of me, public displays of defiance have never really been my thing, and I did feel rather like a sulking child who hasn't got what he wants, but principles are principles.

Dave then made a very public phone call that everyone in the store could hear, during which he explained who he was, where he was calling from and that he had "a customer in his store who had become violent and aggressive to him and the members of his staff and who was refusing to leave the store and so he would like some help please."

There was a pause while he, supposedly, listened to a reply followed by, "Thank you," after which he replaced the handset.

"They're coming to lock you up, arsehole," he shouted in my direction.

At that point I got the impression he was bluffing, so I didn't move. Two can play that game, but after around ten minutes, which was remarkably fast for the local constabulary in that town, two policemen walked in.

"That's him there," said Dave, "he was getting violent and refused to leave."

"No one was getting violent," I said as I got to my feet, "I simply wanted my money back as promised by a member of your staff."

One of the policemen spoke up.

"Let's just go outside shall we, then we can talk to you about what happened."

So off we went out of the store, whereupon I explained the events of the last couple of days, showed them the packaging and the receipt and apologized for them having to come out to deal with such a ridiculous issue.

"Well, you certainly have a point," said the other policeman, "if that is what you were told, then your consumer rights are pretty clear. But we are going to have to ask you not to return to the store for the rest of today, please. Okay?"

"Yes, no problem."

"What I would do is contact their Head Office and speak to someone there. This guy may be following policy, but I would be surprised if the company were that strict."

"Okay—can I go home now?"

"Yes mate—take care now."

There was certainly more chance of me going for a beer with this copper than there was ever going to be with Dave.

Once home I did some research and found the phone number for their Head Office. To my amazement, someone actually answered my call and listened to my experience. They asked me to put everything in writing and send the remote, packaging and receipt to their offices. They told me that Dave's response was not in line with their corporate policy, and someone would be speaking with him. To my further amazement, later that afternoon I had a phone call from a local TV repair company to say that the store's Head Office had called them and requested they send someone round to have a look at my TV. They turned up first thing the following morning, discovered the TV receiver wasn't working—it had nothing to do with the remote—fixed it and said that all their costs were covered.

Around two weeks later, I received a letter from the Head Office apologizing for the way I had been treated and given a store credit to the value of four times the cost of the remote. I gave it a couple more weeks before I went back to the store, and rather than gloat at my final victory, asked to speak to Dave to explain how satisfied I was with the outcome and the response from their Head Office in an attempt to smooth things over.

The lady at Customer Service was the Eastender's enthusiast, who, when I asked after Dave, told me he had been let go. I asked her if she knew what had happened and she said *everyone* new. She added that she had been right about the returns policy, but Dave had always made his own rules up and most of the staff were glad he was gone. Returning stock like that to the manufacturer was too much like hard work for him, so he just used to refuse to take products back. And, apparently, he had been on a final warning as well after he and Doreen had been caught "getting up to mischief" in the storeroom—which certainly *was* against company policy.

"That sounds like something off Eastenders," I said.

She smiled.

A hill called… packaging. It nearly got me arrested, and lost Dave his job.

CHAPTER 4

A Hill Called Jobsworth

The Olympic Gallery at the old Wembley Stadium in west London, England, was an interesting location to watch a great event like a football international, FA Cup Final or the occasional rugby match. But there was one occasion on which it was a challenging place to be.

In July 1999, my wife (at the time) had a sudden and very strong desire to see the Canadian singer, Celine Dion, in concert, mostly because the film *Titanic* had been released two years earlier and Ms. Dion had recorded the theme song. I did not have a sudden or strong desire to see Celine Dion in concert, not then, nor at any time since, but especially not then. She was on a World Tour at the time (Celine Dion, not my wife, which might have been preferable) and was scheduled to play at Wembley Stadium. Despite the wife asking all her friends, no one was interested in attending with her, so as the dutiful husband I agreed to tag along.

At the time, the road structure around Wembley was, for want of a better phrase, something of a challenge, and just getting close was quite an achievement, not to mention finding a place to park. But park we did, in a very large lot with many, many, many other cars. To help cram as many cars into the lot as possible—the drivers of which had all paid a princely sum—there was a team of parking guides ensuring that we were all squeezed in, barely an inch apart, in very close lines. And as one of the first to arrive, we were completely boxed in with absolutely no chance of an early "escape."

Once parked, we joined the throng of concert goers heading to the stadium and the evening's entertainment. This was something of a strange experience for me as every time I had been to Wembley (or any other football stadium) in the past, I had been surrounded by supporters of my team, and supporters of the opposition. This usually created a sense of tribal identity and something of an underlying threat of violence as most football fans of 1990s vintage usually arrived at the game half full of alcohol carrying a hair trigger likelihood that the slightest sign of conflict or disagreement meant they would likely start punching, kicking and generally smashing in the skulls of anyone wearing the opposition's colours.

But this was my first concert of this nature. Having been brought up as a classical musician I was very used to symphony orchestras, opera and a bit of ballet, but Celine Dion was another thing altogether.

The crowd seemed pretty well behaved. There were some other bands performing as the support acts, but it didn't look like their fans were going to kick off in rivalry to Celine's loyal following, so all was well. On arrival at the turnstiles, we showed our tickets and pushed the revolving one-way gate to gain access to the stadium concourse and walked towards our seating section. We headed up some stairs at the top of which there was, for me—usually—one of the most impactful parts of going to a game. Why? A first sight of the beautifully manicured playing surface. The lush green grass, vibrant and immaculately painted white lines and strictly vertical goalposts always made my heart skip a beat. I always liked to arrive early (ask anyone who knows me—I usually arrive early for *everything*), which offered the benefit of being able to see the players come out on to the field and start warming up. Let's face it, you have paid for a seat for the afternoon or evening—why not get as much use out of it as you can?

But this time there was no lush green grass, instead, the hallowed turf had been covered in what looked like aluminium carpet, and thousands of seats. In the centre there was a large square stage raised about ten feet above the ground on the top of which were four sides of very large television screens. We then climbed many, many more steps to get to our designated seats in the far corner of the stadium, a long way from the stage, at which point the realization of the situation finally sank in. Subconsciously, my mind had been playing tricks on me. We were at Wembley; therefore we were going to see some high-quality sport. But there was no field of play, no players, and to be honest, very little excitement.

There was already a band on the stage banging out some tunes.

"Who are this lot?" I asked my wife.

"I don't know," she replied.

"Who are this lot?" I asked the woman sitting next to me, who was clearly enjoying it judging by the gyrating body and hand clapping.

"Mike and the Mechanics," she said, "aren't they amazing?"

"Who?"

"Mike and the Mechanics."

I'd never heard of them and didn't recognize that song, or the next, or the next, or the next. Of course, where we were sitting you could barely make out the band on the stage and had to rely on the large screens above them, on which was broadcast the live concert from cameras situated much closer than we were.

But this came with its own problem.

There was a slight time delay between the live (and distorted) sound that we were hearing from the speakers, and the footage we were seeing, which was very annoying. After a couple more songs I asked my wife what time Celine Dion was on.

"I don't know, but I think there are four more support acts."

"FOUR MORE?"

"I think so."

Celeb In a Basket

It was going to be a long night. But she was right, there were four more bands, none of which I recognized and all of which played songs I had never heard before. Then, about three hours after we had taken our seats, there was a slight lull in proceedings, during which a large wicker basket was wheeled through the crowd in the seats on the aluminium carpet, towards a small door under the stage. I assumed it contained Ms. Dion, otherwise she would have been hiding for a very long time.

The lights then went down, a pre-recorded video of the star act's previous performances started on the big screens and then the main event sprang into life, which, remarkably, was even louder and more distorted than the support acts. But even though I was no Celine Dion fan, I did at least recognize some of the songs in her ninety-minute performance, most notably the theme from the movie *Titanic* ("My Heart Will Go On"), which brought the whole show to its grand climactic close. Thankfully, this meant we could get back to the car and head home.

If only.

Getting out of the stadium was easy enough, and the walk back to the car park was fairly fast, but then our troubles really began. As we had been among the first to arrive, our car was as far from the gate as it was possible to be, and even though there were a lot of cars, things should have been moving faster. We got to our vehicle through a small gap in a fence, which saved us walking all the way round to the main entrance, and realized there was little point in starting the engine or even getting in the seats as no one around us was moving. We stood around and understood it was going to be a very long wait to escape because there were thousands of cars all trying to get out of one exit, and many were now sounding their horns (because that always helps get things moving). There was a lot of tension in the air as people who were actually moving were starting to try to push in front of others—but where were the traffic guides who had ushered us into position when we arrived?

Gone.

And seriously—does it really take *this* long to get cars rolling? We certainly all got *into* the car park much more quickly.

After about forty-five minutes I decided to walk up to the main exit to see what the hold up was, only to immediately realize the problem. When we had arrived that afternoon, there had been two gates open which had allowed double the volume of cars to enter. But now, one of the gates was closed, reducing the exit capacity by 50%. I walked up to the closed gate and tried to open it, only to find there was a long rod stuck in the ground with the top padlocked to the gate so it could not be opened.

Crazy.

Next to the gate was a small hut with a light on inside. I walked up to the door and saw a man sitting inside reading a newspaper with his feet on the desk. I knocked and opened the door.

"Hey mate," I said, "you work here, right?"

"Yep," he said without looking up.

"Do you know why one of the gates is locked shut?"

"They always lock it once everyone is in."

"Why?"

"Dunno."

"Well, if we could open it, it would make life a lot easier, and we could all get out of here and get home quicker."

"Not me."

"Why not you?"

"I'm the night security guy—I'm not going home until seven o-clock in the morning."

"Well at this rate, most of us are not going home until seven o-clock in the morning."

"Not my problem."
"Look, do you have the key for the lock on the gate?"
"It'll be in the desk drawer over there."
"Great, so can we please open it to speed things up?"
"No."
"No?"
"No."
"Why not?"
And then it happened.
"It's more than my job's worth to open that gate."
"What?"
"I said it's more than my job's worth to open that gate. My job is to stop people getting in, I couldn't give a shit about them leaving. Now fuck off."

So, what is a "jobsworth"?

Well, a simple Google search reveals the following:

A jobsworth is a person who uses the (typically small) authority of their job in a deliberately uncooperative way, or who seemingly delights in acting in an obstructive or unhelpful manner. It characterises one who upholds petty rules even at the expense of effectiveness or efficiency.

Related concepts include malicious compliance, passive-aggressive behavior, and micromanagement, which can impair progress through excessive focus on details and obsessive control over that one has authority over.

> *"Jobsworth" is a British colloquialism derived from the notion that something being asked of one in a work environment is too great to risk their job over, as in, "I can't do that; it's more than my job's worth."*
>
> *The Oxford English Dictionary defines it as "A person in authority (esp. a minor official) who insists on adhering to rules and regulations or bureaucratic procedures even at the expense of common sense," as well as a "minor factotum whose only status comes from enforcing otherwise petty regulations".*
>
> *It is a form of passive aggressive obstructionism, using the letter of the law as a weapon to impair progress or prevent change.*

The jobsworth on duty that dark night in west London probably cost me around three hours of my life as it took us over twice as long to get out of that car park than Celine Dion was on stage.

Jobsworths come in many different forms, and we often have to endure their sad little idiosyncratic lives—sometimes at great cost.

They 'Work' Amongst Us

During my consulting career I have had the misfortune to meet with business owners whose workforce had adopted the world of the trade union. Now, before you get all hot under the collar about the value of unions and how bad bosses have used and abused their workforces over the last couple of hundred years, I accept that unions have played an important part in the improvement of working conditions for the average employee. *To a point*, because I have also seen companies get decimated by the jobsworth attitudes of union members.

On one occasion I met with the owner of a company that manufactured very large refrigerator doors for fast food outlets.

These things were about ten feet high by six feet wide and the company had the contract for several large fast-food chains across Canada.

The owner had approached me about doing some work for him in developing the leadership skills of his management team and we met towards the end of a weekday afternoon in his office which overlooked the main production floor. The general discussion included me asking him about the challenges he faced with his business, and, in a perfect world, what changes would he like to make?

The first thing on his list was the deregulation of the union that had formed in his company. I asked what effect this was having on his business and as it was approaching 5:00 p.m. he said he would show me. We walked over to the window that looked down on the shop floor. There were several new doors laid out on benches with four men fastening hinges to the outsides.

"You see those four doors? They are part of a large order of twenty for a customer. The other sixteen are already loaded onto a truck and the whole order must go out tonight or they will be late, meaning we will suffer a financial penalty."

Just as he finished speaking, the shift siren sounded meaning it was the official end of the working day, and all four of the men working on the hinges put their tools down and walked off to head out of the door.

"Okay, so it looks like we have missed the deadline. Let's go and see how far away they are from finishing the job."

We walked down the stairs and over to the benches. Each door had all eight required hinges attached, but in each case, the final two screws were not quite fully tightened.

"There's not even thirty seconds of work left on these doors," he said, "but now we have to wait until the morning because the union shop steward won't allow any of his members to work past the shift deadline. This will cost the company a few thousand dollars in penalties, and I will also have to pay the delivery company for an extra day's work."

"But what's to stop you just finishing the job off yourself—it hardly looks like technical work?"

"Because the last time I did that, when they came in the next day, they 'downed tools' because someone else had done their job for them," he said.

I found it hard to imagine working in that sort of environment.

"Then there was the day when the store man was off sick," he said.

"What happened?"

"Well, as you can see, these guys here are responsible for attaching the hinges and other stuff to the doors once they have been made. Once a door comes from main production, there is a 'demand' notice sent to the store man to provide the rubber seals, door handles and of course, hinges, to these guys.

"He counts them out in the storeroom over there, then brings them over to this work area here, so this lot can attach them.

"But last year, he was off sick for a day, so when this lot came into work, they didn't have any seals, handles or hinges, so they just sat here.

"I came down and told them they could go and get the stuff themselves as it was easy to find, and do you know what one of them said?"

"Go on."

"It's more than my job's worth to do that."

"Really?"

"Yes. He said the union was very clear that we should *only* stick to our own specific jobs and not cover for other people, because if the company sees us doing that, they might start thinking that they can double up jobs and then start to reduce the workforce—so they really believed that it was more than their job was worth to go and get the hinges."

"But couldn't you go and get them?"

"I did—but again they downed tools claiming that I was doing someone else's job, which put that job under threat."

"REALLY?"

"You have *no* idea."

At that point another man walked up to us, and the CEO introduced him as the Chief Financial Officer and his business partner. He asked about the doors and my client explained what had happened.

"It's so crazy," the CFO said, "they don't realize their jobs are under more threat by *not* doing an extra few minutes' work to complete an order, as we are constantly struggling to keep the business afloat, and late deliveries just make it harder to keep the customers we work so hard to get in the first place."

We talked more about the business they started together, and they shared with me that the previous year they had both re-mortgaged their houses just to generate enough capital to meet payroll, but the jobsworth mentality was slowly killing them.

"It is very sad," said the CEO, "as most of the younger guys are really keen and would do a lot more work if they could, but the old dinosaurs are holding them back."

"And they would be financially better off as well," added the CFO, "because we wanted to introduce a dividend scheme, but all the union guys see is corporate profit and refuse to do anything more than what they believe their jobs to be worth."

We talked more about the services I might be able to help them with and we agreed to speak more in the coming months.

No Pay—No Party

I drove away feeling really low as I felt for the employees who clearly wanted to put more effort into their work and who would be better off financially as a result. I also couldn't imagine working in that sort of environment. My background in the military gave me the opportunity to work with people who were willing to go above and beyond what was expected, which created a great sense of mutual accomplishment and *Esprit de Corps*. Yes, we had our share of people who moaned about stuff (I was one of them at times, as we could all be), but generally the working environment was contagious in that we all got stuck in towards a common goal. It was healthy, vibrant and rewarding.

I went on to propose a program for the refrigerator door company that I believed would help their managers in the leadership of their teams, but when it was presented to the workforce, the union representatives insisted they be paid to attend the training (which would have been done during working hours) on top of their regular salaries, which made it financially unviable. About a year later, the owners made the decision that enough was enough and closed the company down, with everyone losing their jobs. I wondered how many of those people stopped to think what their jobs were worth then?

But when it comes to the world of the trade union, for me the strangest example of utter pedantry was while I was doing some work for a performing arts company. They ran three venues: in one of them the staff members were unionized, and in the other two they were not. They had just had a very successful year and the senior leadership team decided to put on a staff appreciation event, which included an evening at one of their locations during which outside catering and staff would be brought in so everyone could attend with a guest. There was a live band, a three-course meal and free bar for the evening, as well as gifts for the partners of staff members. It was a pretty impressive event that looked as generous as anything I had ever seen from an employer, but the union leaders were having none of it.

"If they want us to come into the workplace for an extra evening they should be paying us for our time."

"Hang on, you and your partners are getting a free meal, gifts, live entertainment and a free bar… and you want to be paid for being there as well?"

"Absolutely, it's more than our jobs are worth to be here out of hours and not be paid."

Although the term "jobsworth" is very British, there are other jobsworth stories from around the world.

A few years ago in Sharon Springs, Kansas, USA, a Union Pacific crew boarded a loaded coal train for the long trek to the destination of Salina in New York State. Just a few miles into the trip a wheel bearing became overheated and melted, letting a metal support drop down and grind on the rail; this created a stream of white-hot molten metal droppings that spewed down below the train chassis. A very alert crew member noticed smoke about halfway back in the train and immediately stopped the train in compliance with company regulations. However, the train stopped with the hot wheel over a wooden bridge with creosote ties and trusses. The crew member then contacted the company's Headquarters to request permission to move the train, but when they tried to explain the full situation to the senior manager on duty the request was denied because it was more than his job was worth to allow them to break the rules that prohibited moving the train when a part is defective.

Consequently, the ensuing fire, caused by the molten droppings falling from the train onto the wooden bridge completely destroyed the bridge and the train, meaning that route was inaccessible for more than two years while the bridge was rebuilt. The expense to the company of the loss of the train, plus the bridge rebuild and the additional costs associated with rerouting deliveries ran into many millions of dollars—probably a little more than that manager's job was really worth.

During my career as a military musician, I got to spend a lot of time (and I mean *a lot* of time) travelling on a bus to engagements around the UK and many other countries around the world. This meant dealing with an inordinate number of jobsworths, from car parking officials, security guards and anyone else who filled themselves up with an overwhelming feeling of self-importance and pedantic officialdom.

We always had a lot of equipment to carry around with us, including our instruments, uniforms and large percussion section stuff, as well as our amplification system. Consequently, life was always a lot easier if we could park our transport (bus and truck) as close to the venue, with its stage and changing rooms, as possible.

But those jobsworths were out to get us.

"Sorry, that's as close as you are allowed to get your bus."

"But what about those buses that are parked right next to the building?"

"They were allowed in on someone else's shift—not my problem."

When this form of conversation took place with whomever was at the front of the bus (often our driver) and the car park official, the word "jobsworth" was quickly transmitted back through the band on the bus with an impending feeling of doom knowing our lives were going to get tougher because of this joker.

But it wasn't only the fine British jobsworth that challenged our faith in humanity, because probably the coup de grâce was a certain Italian security guard who worked at the port entrance of the harbour in the city of Naples.

It was September 1999 and I had recently taken up my first senior leadership appointment as the Director of Music of the Band of Her Majesty's Royal Marines, Commando Training Centre. This meant I was in charge of, and responsible for, a band of around fifty musicians. My first engagement in the role involved the band joining up with a large Royal Naval amphibious force to sail through the Mediterranean towards Egypt for a major exercise with ships from more than eighteen other countries, then on through the Bosphorus Strait in Turkey and into the Black Sea.

It was a four-month deployment during which we were required to provide a very wide range of musical support to the thousands of staff members in attendance as well as perform at many official ceremonial events in various countries. We were also due to support a major medical exercise in the Egyptian desert as part of our "secondary" role away from music.

This meant we had *a lot* of kit to carry with us.

The amphibious group of ships from the Royal Navy had sailed from various UK ports during late August but in order for the band to complete its UK summer commitments, we flew out to Naples to join our floating home for most of the deployment: *HMS OCEAN*. This was the Royal Navy's latest helicopter landing platform, and it was a big ship rather like an aircraft carrier which could carry over 1,200 personnel.

Now, the port of Naples offers a few options for ships to berth. One is in the inner harbour, close to the town, and the other is at the very extreme end of the harbour wall—in other words, as far from the port's landside entrance as it is possible to be without being in the sea. As *HMS OCEAN* was larger than all the other ships in the group, she was going to be docked at the end of the harbour wall, meaning it was a long way (around a mile) from the main gate of the port. We had flown out the day before the ships arrived in Naples with all our equipment and had stayed in a hotel just outside the town, which allowed us the opportunity to enjoy the delights of the city for an evening before we joined our ship the next day.

First thing the next morning, we all met in the hotel lobby, and, in true military musician tradition, there were clearly a few hangovers on display. The Italian bus driver designated to collect us from our hotel and take us to our ship—Gino—was remarkably punctual, as was the driver of the truck that would carry our equipment. (You may think my surprise at this is a form of stereotyping, but I had worked in Italy several times before and my wariness was not misplaced.) Once loaded, we were off down the steep hills of Naples towards the port.

It was a beautiful Italian morning, and the view on the way was very impressive, especially as at one point we had to stop for a red light (not something all residents of Naples bother with) and could see the harbour and the ships of the Royal Navy slowly docking in formation, the last of which was *HMS OCEAN* at the far end of the harbour wall. Things were going to plan, and we would soon be onboard and "shaking down" into our accommodation and working spaces.

But then we got to the main entrance to the port, and our first encounter with an Italian jobsworth.

Our bus driver, Gino, seemed like a nice chap, and thankfully spoke enough English to enable us to communicate the basics of a conversation. We pulled up at the security gate and he opened his side window as the guard walked up to the bus and said something along the lines of, "Good morning, we are heading out to *HMS OCEAN* at the end of the harbour wall."

There then followed an exchange in Italian that suggested things were not looking good. After a few minutes of conversation, he turned to me and said we weren't allowed to drive along the harbour wall. Now, this may seem logical if the harbour wall was a small construction that didn't look capable of bearing the weight of a fully laden bus with fifty musicians plus a truck with enough equipment for a four-month deployment.

But in this case, the wall was a rather impressive example of fine Italian civil engineering, to the point where there was a two-way tarmacked road along it right out to the very end. Add to this the fact that right next to where *HMS OCEAN* was now docked, there were several large trucks with supplies ready to be loaded on board, as well as a bus to take the ship's senior officers off to the various ceremonial events that take place the day they arrive in port. I pointed this all out to Gino, who acknowledged the situation and went into round two of trying to convince the security guard of the situation whilst pointing out the large vehicles already alongside our ship.

But he was still having none of it.

The translation revealed that the transport already in place had been allowed out there before this guy had come on shift and, as far as he was concerned, no one else was going to be driving out there that morning. By this time, most of the band had disembarked from the bus (hangovers are generally a little more comfortable in fresh air than on a hot sticky bus) and were watching events unfold.

The Englishman Abroad

My Senior Non-Commissioned Officers (middle managers for want of a better description) were now slipping into action, as it was their responsibility to ensure the logistics of whatever we were doing ran smoothly. But the main problem here was that the guard didn't speak any English, and my team's knowledge of Italian ran to the basic musical terms we dealt with during the execution of our daily work... but there was a lot of muttering of the word "jobsworth" going on.

"What is 'jobsworth'?" asked Gino.

We explained.

"Ah, very good," he replied. "We do not have same word in Italian, but today I learn!"

At this point, tempers were getting a little frayed: it was getting very hot, a lot of people were somewhat hungover, and we were all starting to realize that if we weren't allowed to drive out to the end of the harbour wall, we would have a very serious load carry ahead of us. It was also the point at which the frustrated Englishman abroad reaches a new level in the back-and-forth of the game called communication by restating what he has said several times before, but realizing the recipient does not understand him, repeats it very loudly, and very slowly.

"LOOK… MATE, WE… HAVE… A… LOT… OF… KIT… HERE… WHICH… WE… HAVE… TO… CARRY… ALL… THE… WAY… OUT… TO… THE… END… OF… THE… WALL… SO… STOP… BEING… A… TWAT… AND… OPEN… THE… FUCKING… GATE……….. ***PLEASE***."

The swearing component to this type of request is always interesting because it clearly acknowledges that the other guy doesn't understand you, otherwise it is highly unlikely they will do what you request, but it also adds some substance to the conversation. But it was all to no avail—jobsworth was sticking to his guns. Gino even went into the main gatehouse to see if there was anyone else able to help us, but no, there was not even a supervisor or fellow security guard in attendance.

Our Italian jobsworth was master of his own little piece of authority, and no one was going to take that power away from him.

And so, with an air of utter disbelief and a fair amount of swearing, we unloaded the contents of the bus and truck and my SNCOs put together a strategy that would enable us to load carry everything in our possession in one journey rather than having to go back and forth (we didn't want to leave anything under jobsworth's gaze, and the truck driver had to get to another job very soon).

It was a long way along that harbour wall in that heat with the quality of hangover some of the band were experiencing, but I never heard a single complaint. The whole carry lasted around thirty minutes, and just as we arrived alongside *HMS OCEAN* in a hot sweaty mess, our bus pulled up alongside us, and with a cheery grin on his face, Gino opened his door and shouted, "Hey guys, jobsworth's boss turned up and let me in—what a fucker eh?"

The hill called "jobsworth" is a difficult one to climb when you are on the receiving end of such pedantic behaviour, but I often wonder if the jobsworths themselves ever feel like they are going uphill?

Or maybe they just settle for a life most of us try to avoid.

CHAPTER 5

A Hill Called Passion (in Sports)

*D*epending on your sport, and the team or individual to whom you are committed, life can generally be either happy, or damn miserable. As an enthusiastic follower of the England Rugby and Cricket teams (as well as several other sports and teams), for me, it is generally the latter.

I blame the parents. I mean, pretty much every child of a passionate sports fan is likely going to get introduced at a very early age to the concept that *this* is *your* team for the rest of *your* life. Most professional teams' merchandise stores even sell baby outfits, so they are barely out of the womb before they are all adorned in the team's colours and branding. There are baby-sized replica jerseys, shorts, hats, and other crap, and dad (and mum) will likely decorate their offsprings' bedrooms with team colours and posters of heroes from their own youth. They will be pulled out of the bath and wrapped in the latest club towel. They will go to school with a team backpack and put their pens and pencils in a branded pencil case. What chance do these kids have of ever have opting out in favour of another team?

None.

Of course, if the team is successful and win lots of trophies, life is sweet, and maybe the younger members of the family will one day sit down with dad (and possibly mum) and thank them for choosing such a great team to support. But, if the team generally stinks (and there are more that do than don't), this may be construed as a form of child abuse, because the indoctrination was started early, and there is simply no going back without the risk of a family breakup and the possibility of abandonment.

I was lucky as a child in that while my parents were not particularly passionate about any sport or team, I was given the opportunity to partake in those that took my fancy. My mother had been a respectable cricketer and (field) hockey player in her youth and while serving in the Royal Air Force, and she always instilled in me the importance of "playing to win." A second-place finish was simply earned by the first loser. In my early fifties I took up triathlon and came second in my first ever race, to which my mother commented "room for improvement then."

My dad would take me to see Rotherham United play on the occasional Saturday afternoon and, as I grew up, we went to some floodlit evening games—which always seemed more appealing to me. Rotherham were usually stranded in the third division of the English football league and never won anything, so my expectations were low, but I stuck with them. I wore a red and white scarf to school and always looked out for their results on a Saturday when I didn't go to the game.

But one of the top teams at that time were the mighty Leeds United of Don Revie vintage, and although I was a Rotherham lad, it was acceptable to support the closest top team—so long as it was in Yorkshire—so the Leeds team was on my radar to the point they really became the team I wanted to succeed the most. They won the Football Association (FA) Cup in 1972 and made it back to Wembley for the Final again in 1973 to play a team from the league below them, Sunderland. The game should have been an easy victory for Leeds, but alas, my introduction to tragedy was about to begin. Cup Final Day was special in our house. My mum used to work at the local library on Saturdays, so Dad was in charge (for one day only).

She used to prepare a dinner trolley of "tuck" (a mixture of sweets and chocolate) and cover it with a towel. Once kick off approached my dad would carefully reveal what we had in store that afternoon. And so around 2:00 p.m. on Saturday, 5th May 1973, we settled down to enjoy the pre-match build up, watch the massed military bands entertaining the 100,000 fans (little did I know at the age of nine that my career as a military musician in the Royal Marines would take me on to the Wembley turf on many occasions), and the teams emerge from the famous tunnel behind the goalposts in two lines led by their managers, Don Revie and Bob Stokoe.

The game kicked off, and I was in no doubt that this was going to be an easy victory for the mighty Leeds United, but at the thirty-two-minute mark, Sunderland's Ian Porter collected a loose ball from a corner and struck home the first goal. While this was a bit of a shock, it didn't really raise any alarm bells. Leeds had a team of international superstars in their ranks and the likes of Lorimer, Giles, Bremner, Hunter and "Sniffer" Clarke would soon level things up. But Sunderland had their own hero in the form of their goalkeeper, Jim Montgomery, who pulled off a string of miraculous saves to keep his team in the game and as time passed my expectations turned from hope to despair, then to the realization that Leeds were going to lose.

As referee Ken Burns sounded the final whistle, the dark cloud of defeat descended on our home. My dad wasn't too bothered, he was never really into supporting a team in the first place, but for me it was devastating. We lost. We did not win the FA Cup. We were beaten by Sunderland. That wasn't supposed to happen. This is not good. I didn't really know what to do. There were tears streaming down my face. I left the front room and went and sat on the bottom of the stairs, alone.

My dad came to find me. He asked what was wrong, but I couldn't understand why he was asking me that.

Wasn't it obvious?

He tried to cheer me up by saying it was only a game, which is pretty much the worst thing you can say to someone in those circumstances (I have grown to hate that phrase). It wasn't "only a game," it was way bigger than that.

And so, a very important episode in my life had begun: dealing with losing a game you are passionate about winning.

And to be honest, it's a hill up which I have never stopped running.

The Oxford English Dictionary describes passion as a "strong or overpowering feeling of emotion," and when applied to sport that definition is probably at its most accurate. For most people involved in the commitment of a team, it can be the most important thing in their life. They meet someone, get married and have kids, and while the attachment to those people is obviously important, their sports team is often of a greater value to their very existence.

The wonderful book *Fever Pitch* by Nick Hornby is an autobiographical description of his love for Arsenal Football Club, which started when he was taken to games as a child and carried on into adulthood where his whole life seemingly revolves around the team. The book was made into a film starring Colin Firth and Ruth Gemmell, and then remade into an American version featuring Jimmy Fallon and Drew Barrymore with the Boston Red Socks baseball team in place of Arsenal. But the message is the same: the passion for a sports team rarely matches that of any other.

Alas the balance of wins over losses for most of us is always lopsided to the point where the ship is likely to sink. Losing was something I grew up to loath. I was a terrible loser as a kid (to be brutally transparent—I still am in my sixties), and if I were a kid today, I would probably be submitted to some form of therapy. But that approach also made me want to win. And although I could only control the sports in which I was partaking, the frustration of seeing "my team" fail can be catastrophic.

Only On Netflix

Netflix subscribers may well have come across the series *Sunderland 'til I Die* that documents the trials and tribulations of Sunderland Football Club and its long-suffering supporters in the northeast of England (since beating Leeds in 1973 they haven't done much). The first episode starts with the club having just been demoted from the top division in the English league system and ends with them being relegated to the third division. This results in a significant impact on revenue for the club and many staff members are laid off.

This also has massive ramifications for their supporters, who are now involved in a club that takes them to lower league venues rather than the glory of the big stadiums of English football. The club, which is a huge part of the lives of many people, has seen two seasons of decline. Players and Fans are slipping away from the pinnacle of their sport. They are no longer amongst the "elite" of English football. It must have been tempting for supporters to switch allegiance. To decide to follow an alternate team, a team that is still in the top division, doing well, winning trophies. But that would be treachery. That would be the abandonment of what fans were likely indoctrinated into by their parents.

There are no other options.

The series title, *Sunderland 'til I Die*, is totally appropriate. For these supporters, only death can stop them from physically supporting their team. They will be there through thick and thin. Of course, this is not unique to Sunderland. Pretty much every team sport in the world attracts supporters that are as passionate as the Sunderland gang. Some live in the world of elite competition with their teams continually winning trophies and playing at the top level, and others go through the anguish of failure and relegation. Almost everywhere in the world of sports, this means that if you finish a season at the bottom of a league, you get dumped down a division, and if you finish the top of the division below, you are promoted upwards (the exception is the North American sport system which is franchise-based and has basically "closed" leagues with no promotion or relegation).

In some cases, a team folds completely due to lack of revenue from low attendances, loss of sponsorship deals, and so on. It is generally accepted that you support your local team—I was only aligned with Rotherham because that is where I grew up—but there is a long-standing joke around English football that most people who support one of the world's best-known clubs, Manchester United, have never lived anywhere near Manchester; they just got sucked into supporting a team that won pretty much everything in the 1990s.

Indeed, there is a saying that if you walked around Manchester city centre on match day and it was crowded, United were playing at home, and if it was empty, Manchester City (the other team in Manchester) were playing at home as the locals are generally more likely to support them than jump on the bandwagon of United's success. However, over more recent times, United have struggled and it is City that has risen to the top of English and European football. Of course, some kids have fallen under the spell of success and become City "faithfuls."

For almost twenty years now I have lived near the Canadian city of Toronto. You don't have to spend too much time in Canada to realize how much the population is passionate about their national sport of (ice) hockey and, in this area, sports are all about the Toronto Maple Leafs. The Maple Leafs have won north America's top trophy, the Stanley Cup, thirteen times, but their last success was in 1967—a very long time ago. It is a massive source of frustration for their local supporters, and a massive source of amusement for the supporters of the other teams in the league.

If the promotion and relegation concept were applied to the National Hockey League in the USA and Canada, I fear the Maple Leafs would disappear into the abyss, such has been their form over the years. But, of course, that will never be the case and they will keep playing the other teams, season after season, no matter how badly they perform. You might think the continual failure would lose fans, but, oh no, tickets to Maple Leaf games are hard to get. In fact, the majority of the seats available are held by season ticket holders whose families have held onto them since the original owner was probably witness to the team's successes up to the late 1960s.

I know a few current season ticket owners and they have said, on many occasions, that although the team's continual failure to win the Stanley Cup has tempted them to stop renewing their seats, that would feel like they were betraying their fathers, grandfathers, and in some cases great-grandfathers, who were the original owners.

Those tickets don't come cheap, and neither does a night at a game, given the prices they charge for food and beverages.

The lack of success for teams like the Maple Leafs can also create humour for some. Often when flying into an airport of a city with a notable and successful sports team, a pilot will welcome everyone to the home of the team that won "whatever trophy" recently. I once flew back to Toronto from a business trip and in this case the pilot said, with a pleasant blend of sarcasm and irony "welcome to Toronto—home of the 1967 Stanley Cup Champions."

When it comes to club teams (or franchises), you do, though, have the option of switching allegiance. Although it may not happen often, it is not something you can seriously apply at an international level. My strongest allegiance is to the England Rugby team—but, oh my, have they created some hills for me to climb. In fact, supporting England at pretty much any sport is a seriously demanding task.

While we are the only country in the world to have won the World Cup in football (1966), Rugby Union (2003) and Cricket (2019), each of those victories came with an exorbitantly emotional price tag.

Although I was too young to remember the Football World Cup final that took place when I was three, it is all part of English football history and I have become familiar with the story of the game, the players and the goals. The final against West Germany ended in a 2-2 draw, so it went into extra time, raising the stress levels for everyone involved. England won the game 4-2, but not without a controversial goal-line bounce that to this day is still challenged by many.

International rugby has been, for many years, dominated by Southern Hemisphere nations, notably New Zealand, where the sport is the number one most important pastime (nay religion), South Africa, where it is almost as important, and Australia, where for many years it was right up there, although in recent times its popularity has waned a little. The rugby World Cup began in 1987, is contested every four years and has been won every year by one those countries—except once: 2003 when England won in Australia, with the final played against the hosts.

But, again, this was no easy ride. It was not a victory that was predictable early in the game. Oh no. This was England, in a final, and when the time was up the scores were level and so it was off into extra time. This was another sporting hill of passion for us to endure and, as with 1966, it went to the wire with one of England's finest sporting heroes, Jonny Wilkinson, kicking the winning drop goal with a minute to go on the clock.

Pure theatre?

Pure hell.

And in 2019, England hosted the One Day Cricket World Cup, and again reached the final, to be played against New Zealand, a team that had started to prove it was good at other sports and not just rugby. At the end of the full fifty "overs" each—you guessed it—the scores were level, and it was into the "Super Over."

England won by the skin of their teeth when the New Zealand batsman, Martin Guptill, was run out by inches when sprinting back up the wicket to try and score what would have been the winning run.

Another emotional hill we passionate English sports fans had to run up.

So, we are the only country to have won the world's biggest three team sporting events. But that success must be balanced against the failures. Although England has not reached another final at the football World Cup in almost sixty years, we did reach the European Championship final in 2021 and 2024, but are the only team to have lost them twice in a row.

At the end of the day, it's the hope that gets you.

England's Rugby team have lost in three finals of the World Cup, and our cricket team have also lost in three finals of their World Cup.

Happy days.

Well, Play by The Rules

But of course, there are other hills associated with sporting passion because it isn't just about the challenges of supporting a team, it is also about playing a sport. As a player I started in rugby and cricket. As I developed from a youth player into senior sports, my teams won the occasional trophy or league and got promoted, but we also lost some key finals and tournaments and suffered our fair share of relegations.

And now I am a passionate triathlete in that at the age of sixty I have completed six Ironmans, represented Canada at two Triathlon Age Group World Championships and won a few local races and series titles in my age group. The great thing about Age Group racing is that you are up against athletes who are the same sex and within five years of your own age, so it should be relatively competitive. Probably about half the field are just along for the fun and don't take it too seriously, but not this man. Oh no. I and a lot of others are out for the win—or at least to get on the podium (a word that is officially still a noun not a verb, despite what athletes and commentators keep saying).

The trouble with this is the desire (passion) to finish in the top three means you can go to obsessive lengths to succeed. I am at the stage where the day before a race I will look online at the starting lists and then research past results so I know who I am up against and what their strengths are—which is a little bit pointless, because I can only go as fast as I can go, and I won't impact anyone else's race. I will arrive early to get the best place in the transition area (where we rack our bikes on long metal bars in Age Group sections). I like a spot that is easy to access at the end of the row rather than in the middle where you get tangled up with the rest.

In some races competitors are required to have their age written in marker pen on their right calf so everyone can see who they are racing against and who is in another category, and I have been known to wander around at the start before the donning of wetsuits to get an idea of the competition.

Do they look strong? Are they looking like accomplished swimmers? Are they going to be fast on the bike? Can they run fast off the bike? Again, none of this really matters because even if they were Olympic champions, there isn't much I can do to stop them absolutely thrashing me.

I recently raced in an Olympic distance triathlon (1,500-metre swim, 40-kilometre bike and 10-kilometre run) and when entering Transition 2 (T2—bike to run) saw only one bike in our Age Group row, meaning I started the run in second place. The numbers on the running "bibs" around our waists related to respective age groups, and as there were several "out-and-back" turnarounds on the run course, I would be able to chase down the guy who was leading our race as I would see him coming towards me several times on the switchbacks.

By the time we got to the 5-kilometre mark, I caught and passed him, putting me in the lead. All I had to do then was keep my pace and not "blow up" by running too fast. But as I approached the 8-kilometre mark, I noticed a runner who looked my age or so at one of the turnarounds. He was getting closer to me, but he wasn't wearing a bib number, which technically meant he should be disqualified. Should I assume he was in my category and push harder at the risk of burning out all my energy and struggling to finish? Or should I assume he was younger than me? Or maybe a Race Official would spot the misdemeanour and disqualify him, meaning I should stick to my pace. I chose the latter and kept to my speed, only to be passed a few metres from the finish. I discovered a few moments later that he was indeed in the same category, he had not been spotted by an official and he was awarded first place.

He didn't show up later for the presentations and the guy in third, who had also noticed the "winner" hadn't been wearing his bib, suggested we should challenge the result and propose his disqualification, promoting us to second and first respectively. It was a relatively small event that wasn't part of a qualifying process for anything, so I just felt at the time that we would probably have been seen as a little bit pedantic had we complained, and the officials (who were usually very sharp on all aspects of the regulations) had clearly not been doing their jobs (they were also volunteers who were giving up their weekend as well), but did it really matter?

Well, in hindsight, yes it did. Because I have since regretted not making a claim against the "winner."

I can sense a certain amount of eye rolling from you, dear reader, at this point. But I am sure some of you would indeed have complained about the result and demanded justice. I also feel that had it been me not wearing my bib number, I would either have been disqualified, or on exiting T2 been sent back to get it, costing me valuable seconds and possibly the race.

You see, this passion for sport really is a steep hill to climb.

But how much are we willing to suffer for our passion?

There are those who are there just for the enjoyment of being part of an event. They may train just to ensure they are able to finish the race and get their medal and T-shirt, but they don't really care whether they are in the top ten in their age group or finish last.

Good luck to them.

But then there are those who compete. They are out to win, or at the very worst, come second or third. And there are those who also set themselves specific goals, such as beating their times from previous years etc. I am never going to win an Ironman triathlon. And I don't mean the overall race, I mean within my age group. I have managed to get into the top ten on the odd occasion but winning and getting to the Holy Grail of Ironman—the World Championships in Kona, Hawaii—is not going to happen no matter how hard I train. I'm just not built for that level of performance. But just completing six full Ironman races is satisfying enough for me, and my race is more about seeing if I can better my previous best times as I get older, than it is about beating guys who are just wired differently.

I am competitive at shorter local races and have many race medals from winning or coming in the top three in my age group. But this is just another hill to climb. I don't just turn up for that local Sprint or Olympic distant race with the objective of finishing, I turn up with the goal of beating the other guys. This means I must take the race much more seriously rather than just turning up and having a go. I need lots of sleep in the days leading up to the race, so no late nights. The correct nutrition plan requires some sacrifice as the intake of chocolate (my Achilles Heel) must be reduced considerably, and of course I must follow a concerted and disciplined approach to training, generally very early in the mornings.

Is that a hill worth climbing?

Well, if I come away from a race having won, or finishing in the top three, then yes, I think it is.

The Privilege of Sacrifice

I recently came across a fascinating cycling documentary called *Wonderful Losers: A Different World*[6]. It is based on what are known as "domestiques" in the world of road racing. Domestiques are part a team of up to eight cyclists and their job is to support the designated riders who have different areas of specialization. One will be the nominated leader, another the hill climb specialist, and another a sprinter who shines over the last few hundred metres of a flat stage or one-day race. The domestiques are tasked with riding in the wind to shield the team leader so they can ride in the slipstream they create (called "drafting" off them), and to make steep climbs easier so they have enough energy to ride away from the opposition for the win.

A domestique may be required to form a "train" in order to ride hard and deliver their sprinter near the finish of a race so they have been "pulled" along in the slipstream and can dash ahead for the win. They may also be required to go back and forth to their team cars and deliver food and drink to their teammates—a task that requires huge levels of fitness and stamina. And they are often involved in crashes, the bane of all competitive cyclists, as their job is to protect the stars on the roster. But the interesting thing about domestiques is that they never win a race. They are not supposed to. It is their job to ride for the team leaders, climbers and sprinters.

---

[6] Arunas Matelis, director, *Wonderful Losers: A Different World*. Released: 2018. Available at Vimeo on demand.

The documentary is described as:

"The first time in over 40 years an independent filmmaker outside of the broadcast networks has been allowed to film behind the scenes in an exclusive insider look at the notorious and celebrated Italian Grand Tour Cycling race, the Giro d'Italia.

Filmed over several years, Arūnas Matelis and his crew joined the medic teams to reveal the unseen footage of the riders at the back of the race—the so-called "water carriers," "domestiques," "Gregarios"—who forego their careers and personal victories for the sake of victory for their leader.

Its heroes are athletes undertaking the most difficult challenges, while remaining in the shadow of leaders, without the right to personal victory.

Through their sacrifice, they pave the way to victory for the band's stars, becoming a universal symbol of sacrifice."

One scene features a domestique who had recently been involved in a high-speed crash during a multi-day road race. His shoulder was badly damaged, as was his knee and he had a lot of "road rash," the deep grazing that occurs when you fall off a bike on a hard road while travelling at a very high speed wearing only thin Lycra, down the side of his body. There was no question of him quitting the race as he was a vital component of the team's strategy and would be required to contribute on each of the remaining nine days of the race.

In the scene, he is on the treatment table on the evening of the crash getting a massage, which, judging by the groaning, and the look on his face, suggested he was in a lot of pain and was seriously suffering. His Directeur Sportif (team manager) was next to him and asked him an interesting question:

"How much are you willing to sacrifice for your passion?"

The answer: "Enough to ensure I don't give up and quit the race."

"Exactly. Remember: Sacrifice is a privilege."

Which got me thinking.

Climbing up the hill called sporting passion can be hard work. But how much am I willing to sacrifice for my passion? I spent some time thinking back to my life in sport for some notable examples. Training for and completing an Ironman triathlon comes at a price, especially if it is your first attempt. You can't cheat (well, maybe you can—see Chapter 6). You have to put the work in. You have to get out there and train hard. For me the biggest challenges were the long weekly rides. My plan, which has worked well over the years, includes, amongst many other things, a long bike ride each week of at least six hours, for eight to ten weeks in the buildup to the race and I doubt there are many Ironman triathletes out there who do much less than that.

When searching for sacrifice in an endurance sport you don't have to look far, but what about my previous life? There is one occasion that I believe typifies this. Some of my happiest years as a rugby player took place during my twenties while representing the local club in a small town called Deal on the Kentish coast of Southeast England. This was where I joined the Royal Marines Band Service as a sixteen-year-old in 1979 and although I was drafted to other parts of the country on several occasions once I was fully trained, I also served back at the base in Deal during three other periods of my career. We played in the Kent leagues, which meant games every Saturday, sometimes a cup game on Sunday and occasionally a floodlit game on a Wednesday evening. As well as the games, we had biweekly training on Mondays and Wednesdays, the first of which was often a real struggle as we were usually still in a lot of pain from the games at the weekend.

I still vividly remember one Monday evening in late January when we were due to train but the weather was brutal. Deal is on the corner of the Kent coast close to where the English Channel meets the North Sea. Winds can be ferocious and on this Monday evening there was something close to a gale coming in off the sea and hitting our clubhouse and changing rooms. We had suffered a heavy defeat in the Kent Cup to a team from London the day before and were all hurting, mentally and physically. We had a dedicated training ground away from our match day pitch so that we wouldn't damage the regular playing surface while training, but by this stage of the season it wasn't showing a single blade of grass and was instead around ankle deep in mud. The rain was torrential, but the wind was so strong it wasn't coming down, instead it was blowing the rain almost horizontally across the field. Our training flood lights were on, but the posts they were fastened to were being buffeted so much it was more like being in an open-air disco than a rugby club training ground.

My teammates and I were all sitting in the changing room feeling much the worse for wear after the weekend. It was cold and damp, the wind was howling, the rain was beating against the window, and all we wanted to do was go home and sit in front of the fire. There was a hope amongst us that our coach, Gerry Moore, might take pity and decide that a night off would probably benefit us more than a couple of hours out there. But no: a couple of moments later he appeared at the door all dressed up in about four layers of Gortex, a thick woolly hat, gloves and waterproof boots.

"Come on," he shouted, "we aren't going to win any fucking games sitting in here!"

So out we went to make a sacrifice in support of our passion for rugby.

The hill called passion in sport can be a tough one at times.

But there can also be occasions when passion turns to hate.

While hate is a strong word, there aren't many things in my life I can honestly say I have truly hated. Ingrown toenails and kidney stones spring to mind, and the incorrect use of apostrophes, but I would generally describe the hills I have had to climb as annoying, irritating, frustrating and so on, but really not things I "hate."

There have, though, been times when it has been hard *not* to hate the Welsh.

Although born in England, my mum had attended school in South Wales as her father was an officer in the Royal Artillery and was stationed just outside Swansea. She was the eldest of five children and three of her four brothers were born in Wales. And oh my, did they take that seriously. It may sound a little hypocritical when I, as a died-in-the-wool Yorkshireman, scoff a little about someone making a big thing about where they were born, but at least my dad was also born in God's own county, whereas my three Welsh uncles had English parents and an English brother and sister.

And as I got to know one uncle in particular, it became apparent that there were times when he didn't like the English very much. He always made a big deal of phoning us when Wales beat England at rugby (which happened a lot in the 1970s), and when we saw him and his family, he would keep harping on and on about the "posh and arrogant English snobbery."

I didn't take a lot of notice of it all growing up and came to respect the wonderful talents of some great Welsh rugby players such as Gareth Edwards, Phil Bennett, JPR Williams, Ray Gravell and Derek Quinnell. The last two played for my uncle's local club, Llanelli, and on one occasion whilst visiting them he took me into the clubhouse after a game where I got to meet them and some other notable players. Some of them seemed like nice guys, but one of them asked me where I was from, and when I told him he laughed and told me to "fuck off back over the border," to much cheering from the locals.

Sit Down and Shut Up

Undeterred, I still found hate hard to come by, until I went to my first England versus Wales rugby match at Twickenham, in London.

It was the mid-1980s and England were starting to become a much stronger team. They had beaten Wales a few times, which was hard for them to swallow, and most of the other teams in the Five Nations tournament (Scotland, Ireland and France) judged their season not just on winning the tournament, but on beating England. In fact, they could lose every other game, but victory over England would generally redeem their season overall.

On this occasion I and a couple of mates had tickets in the West stand and as we took our seats, I noticed an elderly lady sitting behind us with what looked like three grandchildren, all decked out in Welsh colours. I smiled at them, and grandma gave me a look that would likely curdle milk. The kids looked like they wanted to punch me. During the singing of the respective national anthems, she and the kids belted out the Welsh anthem, *Land of My Fathers* with impressive gusto, but when it came to God Save the Queen, she told them to sit down rather than show any respect. "You *never* sing this, kids, remember that—*never!*" she barked at them.

Once the game kicked off, she turned into something akin to a rabid dog, hissing and shouting about every aspect of the game and screaming how the ref was blind if he awarded a decision to England, and he was brilliant if he did likewise to Wales. It was hard to endure and at half time, with England narrowly in the lead, she proceeded to tell the grandkids how the English arrogance was going to be seriously damaged in the second half. It wasn't, as we went on to win. But one moment really bothered me.

There was a point in the play when the England flanker, Peter Winterbottom, made a tackle and was trapped at the bottom of a ruck (a pile of players and generally a nasty place to be) when Grandma leapt to her feet and started yelling, "stamp on his head, gouge his eyes out—KILL THE ENGLISH FUCKER," to which one of my mates turned around and told her to sit down and shut up.

She didn't.

She just got worse as the game drew to a close, at which point we all turned round to see her grandkids stick two fingers up at us as grandma tapped them on their heads and told them it was time to get the hell out of England and go home.

English hating is quite a passion among many of the Welsh. There is one classic tale of a Wales versus England game in the early 2000s. The England team were travelling to the stadium on their official bus, and as they moved slowly through the streets of Cardiff, were surrounded by supporters of both teams. One Welsh supporter was so consumed with hatred that he ran into the road and up to the stationary bus, and head butted it.

The Scots aren't much better. Many of them will tell you they support two teams: Scotland and anyone who is playing against England.

If there was a major football tournament taking place that involved the home nations in addition to England, I would generally have supported Scotland or Wales as well. That is until I was in Scotland during a Football World Cup and went into a pub to watch England play Germany. Apart from the language, it would have been easy to assume I was in Berlin, Frankfurt or Dusseldorf, such was the anti-English vitriol on display. Indeed, most of the locals were wearing German football shirts and the pub was adorned with German flags. Apparently, they did that every game England played, although it is always amusing when England stays in a tournament a long time thinking about all the shirts and flags of the countries England are playing those Scots have to buy. It will cost them a fortune if England get to a final.

And this isn't just a British sport occurrence. There are many examples of other places around the world where passion and hatred are barely indistinguishable. Spanish football and games between giants like Real Madrid and Barcelona. The great south American clubs and countries, and of course India versus Pakistan at cricket, with over a billion people stopping to tune in (eat your heart out, Superbowl, if you think you are the biggest sporting event on the planet).

But of course, the hatred doesn't extend to everyone, and I have some very close friends who are Welsh and Scots. They want their teams to win, and the competitiveness is generally done in good spirit, and no matter the winner, we share a handshake and a few beers and move on.

But when you are so engrossed in a team, or a sport, or the desire to win fairly…

… a hill called… passion in sport can be a tough one to climb at times.

CHAPTER 6

A Hill Called Sporting Cheats

It was about 5:30 a.m. on the morning of Sunday, January 29, 2023, and I was standing on a street in downtown Miami, Florida surrounded by about 16,000 people.

It was the start of the Miami Marathon and Half Marathon. I was training for the London Marathon around three months later and, living through a Canadian winter, was keen to do a "warm-up" race in more favourable climes, so had headed south for the weekend. As with most races with such a large number of participants, there were a series of starting corrals, where one was supposed to wait with runners who had registered for the race with a predicted finish time, the aim being that you would be starting and running with people with a similar pace to your own. But unfortunately, there are always some people who are either ultra-ambitious or clueless and rather than setting off at and maintaining a reasonable speed, one finds them, instead, walking down the centre of the road within ten minutes, consequently getting in everyone's way.

As with all races, we were wearing our "bib" number—a piece of specially manufactured paper designed to withstand all sorts of abuse (water, endurance drinks, energy gels, sweat and other bodily fluids)—for the duration of the race and beyond (if you want an additional souvenir). The bib displays your unique race number, some sponsor branding, and sometimes your name, which encourages spectators to shout it out in support of your efforts. It also has a timing chip encased in protective material attached to the back which sends a signal to the timing mats at the start line, finish line and various other places. This ensures runners do not take short cuts and must (supposedly) complete the full course. It also allows for runners to be "tracked" so their whereabouts on the course is known by their family and friends. The main aim of the timing chip is to reduce cheating: if you don't register with each timing mat you could, if caught taking a shortcut, be disqualified.

The atmosphere at the start of the Miami race was intense, with loud music and a Master of Ceremonies who didn't appear to have much confidence in the Public Address system to the point he was shouting so loudly my ears were crackling. I looked around me and there really were a lot of runners, most of whom had fastened their race bibs to the front of their shirts with safety pins or small magnets (which are rubbish—don't waste your money), but next to me was a guy wearing a number "belt." This is a thin strip of material encircling the waist that has two small lines of elastic on it that end with toggles which hold your bib number in place. Although it can be worn for just running, it is mostly used for triathlon competitors, enabling athletes to quickly put their number on after the swim or bike leg so they don't have to faff around with safety pins, etc. For some reason, I glanced down at the guy's race number to see he did not have one bib on his belt, but four.

"What's with the four bibs?" I asked him.

"Oh, this is how we qualify for Boston every year," he said with a big grin on his face.

The Boston Marathon is an annual race hosted by several cities and towns in greater Boston in eastern Massachusetts, United States. It is traditionally held on Patriots Day, the third Monday of April. Begun in 1897, the event was inspired by the success of the first marathon competition in the 1896 Summer Olympics. It is the world's oldest annual marathon and ranks as one of the world's best-known road racing events. The Boston Marathon is open to runners eighteen or older from any nation, but it is not a race you can just enter at will: runners must secure a spot by first completing a standard marathon course certified by a national governing body affiliated with World Athletics within a certain period of time prior to the desired Boston Marathon (usually within approximately eighteen months). Qualifying times are based on age groups in five-year increments, with women allowed a longer time than men, and it is no mean feat to get the required time if you are no better than an average runner. Even if you make the qualifying time, there is no guarantee you will get a place as race organizers will pick the fastest qualifiers for however many slots there are available in each age group category. As a consequence, there is a fairly high level of kudos given to any runner who "Boston Qualifies."

"What do you mean, this is how you qualify for Boston?" I asked.

"We get into teams of four. One of us starts with the belt and the four bibs, runs a hard ten kilometres, then meets the next guy at a designated point, hands over the belt, then the next guy runs ten kilometres and so on until the last guy gets to forty kilometres where we meet to get our own bibs back to run the last two kilometres on our own so we cross the finish line separately."

So basically, it was almost impossible to catch them cheating because their bibs and the timing chips would all register with each of the timing mats. Then they would all cross the finish line, where they would all get photographed—as individuals. And with so many runners, it is entirely usual for large groups of timing chips to cross the on-course mats at the same time, so they were unlikely to raise any suspicion.

"Holt shit," I said, "how long have you been doing that?"

"For about five years," he said, "there are loads of us who come up from Mexico every year since the City of Mexico Marathon started disqualifying runners for cutting the course."

Which reminded me of the last time I was there.

In 2018 I was doing some work in Mexico City, and after returning from a run early one morning got chatting to the hotel concierge, a young man from New York who was also a keen runner. He asked if I had been in town for the marathon the previous week. I hadn't, but he told me there had been a lot of runners disqualified for course cutting, and whilst doing some research for this book I discovered a report from the New York Times that stated that in 2017, 5,806 runners had indeed been disqualified for course cutting, and in 2018, 3,080 were disqualified for the same reason.[7]

How Do They Sleep at Night?

When I looked around the corral in Miami, I counted at least twenty runners with belts carrying multiple bibs, which meant there were at least eighty "Boston Qualifiers" cheating that day.

I was astonished—or maybe I was being naïve.

Their strategy seemed so simple—but surely it couldn't feel right qualifying for a race that so many people train so hard to get into?

"We don't care—if *we* don't cheat, someone else will," the runner said. "Some of my friends earn good money every year as bib mules for Boston Qualifiers."

"Bib mules?"

"Yeah—people enter a race, collect their bibs, then hand them to a faster runner they've hired to complete the course, so they qualify and get to Boston. The going rate is around $300."

---

[7] Source: New York Times: September 6. 2023 By Amanda Holpuch and Víctor Manuel Ramos. https://www.nytimes.com/2023/09/06/sports/mexico-city-marathon-cheating.

"Hold on—people *hire* fast runners to carry their bib around a course, so they qualify for Boston?"

"Sure—happens all the time. Why would you put yourself to all that trouble to qualify when you can pay some young fast guy to do it for you?"

"Because it's wrong, and it clearly prevents a lot of genuine and honest runners from having the opportunity to get to Boston."

"Who cares about them? They clearly aren't very clever if they don't do stuff like this to get to Boston," he said.

We had been in our corral for almost an hour before we finally began moving towards the start. But even when we did move, it was only for a few metres at a time before we stopped and then started again. There was clearly a hold-up of some sort. But as we approached the start (and the *really* loud music) we could see loads of runners cutting in front of us through a gap in the fence that had been forced open, so rather than wait around in corrals with everyone else, they just pushed in at the front.

They were, in effect, cheating before the race had even started.

The route took us in a northerly direction before turning right to head towards South Beach, but on the inside of the turn, there was a park, which—you've guessed it—many runners were cutting through to shave off a few metres rather than go all the way to the corner. As with most inner-city races, there were lots of side streets for people to cut through, and that day many people were, which really started to leave a sour taste in my mouth.

Why enter a race and then cut the course?

How can people take a medal at the end of a race they have not properly completed?

How can you cheat and effectively stop an honest runner from qualifying for something like the Boston Marathon?

Even though the race left me feeling quite demoralized, I returned to do it again in 2024, but this time my frustration was realized at the finish line.

Pretty much every race provides "Finisher" medals to participants who "complete" the course, and these are handed out just after runners cross the finish line by volunteers who are usually holding armfuls of them. There are usually large racks of medals behind the volunteers as a means of resupply to ensure there is not a "bottleneck" of people waiting to collect them, but in 2024, there was a very long lineup of runners just beyond the finish. It quickly became apparent there were no lines of volunteers, or racks of medals. Instead, there was one person handing out medals over an eight-foot fence, one at a time, and rather than wait their turn, many people were just pushing around the outside of the main throng to snatch one out of his hand. It was chaos, and took almost an hour for me to collect what I had earned and head to the exit, during which I asked a volunteer why they had changed the medal process from the previous year?

"Last year we had a lot of people stealing handfuls of medals off the volunteers and the racks, and we ran out before everyone had finished."

It isn't surprising they ran out if people were helping themselves to as many medals as they wanted. This would also explain why there were race staff in the middle of the road during the last few hundred metres checking people had their bibs as apparently there had been instances of "runners" joining the route just before the end in order to claim a medal.

So even people who weren't in the race were cheating.

Further investigation into the subject of race cheating led me to an interesting, if not somewhat alarming, website: marathoninvestigation.com.

This is mainly a blog site that reports on research into races and individuals who are suspected of cheating. Its subject matter includes marathons, triathlons and ultra running (long races of fifty or even 100 kilometres or miles) and it appears rather like a rogues' gallery of guilty "athletes" who have been caught, plus analyses of certain races where statistics are somewhat "suspect."

Shortly after the 2017 Mexico City Marathon, they received requests to review the results. A Facebook page was created by disgruntled athletes outing many alleged cheaters and there were many comments that there were thousands of runners cutting the course. The writers were skeptical at first, however, when they looked at the results, and the paces, the data seemed to support the claim that an unprecedented number of missed mats were widely attributable to runners cutting the course.

There were eight intermediate timing mats on the course, one roughly every five kilometres.

What did the data show? It showed that 36% of all runners missed at least one mat and 23.5% of all runners missed multiple mats.

Next, they analyzed which timing mats were missed—possibly there was a technical issue with a couple of timing mats that would explain this data. This distribution is interesting. The highest number of runners missed the early mats. Only 4% of the runners missed the final mat—just 2.3 kilometres (1.4 miles) short of the finish line. All other mats were missed by a minimum of 10% of all runners.

They then analyzed those who completed the run and became "Boston Qualifiers," which is the most alarming statistic of all. They discovered that a total of 3,942 "Boston Qualifiers" had missed at least one mat, with some missing as many as eight. This shows an even more distinct pattern than that of the entire field. If the data picked up by the mats is accurate, many runners crossed the starting line, jumped off the course and jumped back in towards the end. The paces calculated by the timing splits confirm this. For most of the runners with multiple missed splits, the data shows unreasonably fast splits where data is missing.[8]

---

[8] Source: marathoninvestigation.com: No Shortage of Imposters at the Boston Marathon.

When you consider the Boston Marathon field is around 22,000, the cheaters at the 2017 City of Mexico race would have made up 18% of the field. And that is only one race.

How many runners cheat at other races? How many do the multiple bib trick? How many hire bib mules? How many runners at Boston are genuine qualifiers and what percentage have cheated to get there?

Reading this reminded me of an instance at the London Marathon in 2001—my first race at that distance. At that time, there were fewer timing mats, basically just at the start, the halfway point and the end, and there was a report a few weeks after the race, of a runner who took just over two hours to complete the first half but then broke the World Half Marathon Record by more than fifteen minutes for the second half of the course. When challenged, he claimed he suddenly "felt a wave of energy and simply flew around the route," although shortly afterwards he retracted this claim and admitted he had jumped over a railing under a dark underpass.

And the Boston Marathon itself is not immune to cheating: in 1980, Rosie Ruiz crossed the finish line first in the women's race. However, marathon officials became suspicious, and it was discovered that she did not appear in race videotapes until near the end of the race, with a subsequent investigation concluding that she had skipped most of the race and blended into the crowd about 800 metres (half a mile) from the finish line, where she then ran to her false victory. She was disqualified eight days later, and Canadian Jacqueline Gareau was proclaimed the winner, although sadly she did not get to enjoy the race-day celebrations as a true winner should.

There are also many examples of fake Boston Marathon bibs, where people have created their own bibs with someone else's number on them, started and ran the race, collected their medals and even had the audacity to show their photographs on social media, where they have often been caught. On the Marathon Investigation website there are examples of genuine runners sharing photographs of others with the same number with comments such as "hang on, she's wearing my bloody bib number!"

And I Thought He Was 'Clean'

Of course, cheating in sport is not a 21st century trend, and a look back in history reveals numerous tales of sporting vagabonds and ne'er-do-wells; more recently the well-documented life of American cyclist Lance Armstrong is probably amongst the most well-known examples.

And it was this that really affected me the most when it comes to the impact sporting cheats have had on my life.

As with most triathletes, I have a very keen interest in cycling, certainly more than I do in the other disciplines of swimming and running, and I was fascinated by the story of Lance Armstrong, a very good athlete who was diagnosed with testicular cancer, but who then overcame the disease and returned to bike racing and went on to "win" the Tour de France on seven consecutive occasions. However, throughout these victories there was always a suspicion of doping, driven by many eminent journalists. But I was totally hooked in by the Lance Armstrong bug. I bought his autobiographical books, his yellow Livestrong bracelets and promotional clothing, as well as his team cycling clothing when he rode for the US Postal and Discovery Channel teams. He was, for want of a better description, my hero, and I defended him on many occasions when his aura of cycling excellence was challenged either to me directly or on social media.

How could someone who has faced so much adversity in life succumb to such nefarious tactics in order to win?

Don't performance enhancing drugs screw your body up, especially when you are so vulnerable after the impact of cancer treatment?

As the true story of his cheating came to light, there was an ever-increasing number of whistle-blowers sticking their heads above the parapet, with the likes of former teammates Tyler Hamilton and Floyd Landis going public with their version of events that had occurred while riding in support of Armstrong, all pretty much indicating there was a bullying and control freak environment within the team. I still wasn't convinced and put them, and the likes of Travis Tygart, CEO of the US Anti-Doping Agency (and chief investigator into the claims against Armstrong) in the category of lying shits who were out for self-promotion and fame.

Eventually it seemed inevitable that his cover was blown and in January 2013 it was reported that he was going to appear on Oprah Winfrey's TV show to confess to his sins. Even then I didn't believe it but tuned in (for the first and last ever time) to her show. There he was, and out came his confession.

Yes, he doped to all of his Tour de France "victories."

Oh Lance, Lance, Lance……. how could you do this to me? I have defended you for more than a decade and now you tell me it was all a lie? Within minutes I was scouring my house for anything associated with Lance Armstrong. His books, the yellow bracelets, cycling jerseys, Livestrong clothing—I put it all into a garbage sack and out on the street for collection. What I nearly added was my faith in honesty and fair play. I truly did not understand how someone could knowingly and strategically go ahead and dominate a sport through cheating.

And what was ironic was his association with the sports brand Nike, because they have become, for me, synonymous with cheating after they "rewarded" the American sprinter Justin Gatlin with a $15,000,000 sponsorship deal when he returned to athletics after not one, but two doping bans.

What message does that send to young sports-people?

Cheating comes in many forms, and not just race qualifying and doping.

I emigrated to Canada in 2005 at the age of forty-two, and despite having not really played any serious sport for more than a decade (my body was pretty weary after many years of rugby) decided I should make an attempt to "turn native" and get into the national sport of ice hockey (henceforth known simply as "hockey").

I could skate. Well, I thought I could, but in reality, growing up in South Yorkshire, ice skating usually meant as a teenage lad, getting on a bus from Rotherham to Sheffield with my mates, heading to the "Silver Blades" ice rink, where we would rent a pair of antiquated skates (which had blades that were more rusty than silver) and wobble around the ice in the same anti-clockwise direction for an hour trying not to fall over and make fools of ourselves in front of any girls. Then it was off for a "Chip Butty," (a bread roll filled with greasy French fries) and back home on the bus.

But, having attended a few games of professional hockey, I realized there was probably a bit more to it than that, so I signed up for a twelve-week Adult Beginners Hockey Course at 9:00 a.m. on Saturday mornings. I thought a pair of skates and a stick would be enough equipment to get started, but no, we had to go "full-on protection" in order to join the course, so it was off to the local hockey shop to invest in the whole gamut of paraphernalia.

Having spent a lot of my rugby playing days scoffing at the amount stuff American footballers wear in the NFL, I was bit apprehensive at having to don helmet, shoulder, elbow, knee and shin pads, as well as very thick gloves, but quickly realized there was an almost certain eventuality that you are going to hit the boards (solid barriers around the ice that *do not* move under *any* circumstances) and glass (Perspex screening that sits on top of the boards) and of course the ice, on regular occasions, often when travelling completely out of control at a frighteningly high speed.

The course taught basic skills that looked simple in theory (skating forwards, stopping quickly, turning sharp left and right, and skating backwards), but never in my life had the phrase "you can't teach an old dog new tricks," been more appropriate. Add to that the challenge of controlling a puck and passing it to teammates while working out where you are supposed to be to receive it back, or how to take it off the opposition. The sessions were fun and mostly made up of adult immigrants like me who were trying to "integrate" into the Canadian way of life. And of course on completion of the twelve-week programme, we were invited to take our hockey to the "next level" (for me, the only way *was* up), which involved signing up for the local 'Safe' Hockey League, an in-house recreational team competition where players were placed in leagues from level A (really good amateurs) to level E (supposedly crappy beginners and those who have played for years without managing to get any better).

Describing hockey as "safe" is something of an oxymoron as you will always have twelve players on the ice travelling at various speeds, but the essence of this form of the game was that it was supposed to be played with minimum physical contact, compared to the professional game, during which players are constantly "checking" their opponents into the boards, or smashing them so hard they get airborne and land very heavily on the ice. Of course, they have all been conditioned to play the game in this way as they have developed as young players who graduate to the professional ranks, but for the rest of us, the 'Safe' Hockey League was a version of the game that would allow us to enjoy the sport without the dangers of serious physical injury.

The league was based on a series of twelve games played once a week on a round-robin format, and my team were due to play on Monday evenings. I was allocated to a team in the E Division (only because there was not an F Division) and we were allowed a one-hour team training session a week out from the first game. We turned up with all our equipment whereupon we did introductions, during which I was to find out, to my horror, that I was the only one who was a complete novice. Most had been playing the game since their youth, and this was a chance to play to a very low standard rather than with much better players. One of the team members was in his twenties, and his father was a coach who agreed to come along and take charge by allocating our "lines." Hockey teams have six players on the ice at any one time: a goalkeeper, two defencemen and three forwards. I was to learn that it is a remarkably fast and high-intensity sport where players are usually limited to a couple of minutes on each "shift." There are usually three "lines" of defence and four "lines" of forwards constantly rotating throughout the game.

The better player you are, the more likely you are to be on the first or second "line."

I was a forward (left wing) on the fourth line, where it was suggested by our coach that I would cause the "least amount of damage to our chances of winning."

We all returned the following week for the first of our twelve games in the E Division of the 'Safe' Hockey League for that part of the year. We were handed our team jerseys, a nice blend of yellow and black, and our coach confirmed our "lines," and the fact I hadn't been promoted from the previous week (which was quite a relief, to be honest). Once fully adorned in all the equipment (I still wasn't convinced we needed to wear it all—this was "safe" hockey, right?) we were soon out on the ice to warm up ready for the start, or the 'Puck Drop' to use the officially-recognized terminology.

Our first lines of defencemen and forwards were ready to go while the rest of us settled on the bench, like coiled springs, ready to leap into action when called upon. The first three shifts went by fairly quickly, until there was a stoppage in play and our coach called out "Fourth Line out you go."

This was it. My time had arrived.

Oxygen: Kind Of Important

After all the upheaval of emigrating from the UK to Canada, getting set up in a new home, starting a business and beginning the integration into a completely new way of life in a new country, it was time to feel truly Canadian by making my first contribution to the game of hockey—albeit in a safe environment rather than the more traditional form involving various levels of legalized brutality. I was up off the bench and over the boards careful not to lose my balance and end up on my back looking like the complete novice I was. I slowly skated out to my position on the left wing. The game was about to restart with a face-off, where the puck is dropped between a player from each team while the rest remain outside a defined circle on the ice. I was next to my direct opposite number (their right wing) on the edge of the centre circle. Everyone was bent over at the waist with the flat part of the bottom of their sticks on the ice, so I did the same.

My opposite number, with whom I was now shoulder-to-shoulder with on my left, turned his head to look at me.

"First game?" he asked.

"Yes," I replied.

"Where are you from?"

"England."

"I fucking hate the English," he said just as the referee dropped the puck to restart play. At the same moment he swung his stick away from me, then, with what must have been as much force as he could possibly muster, rammed the butt-end into my ribcage. Now, hockey equipment is reasonably substantial, and includes shoulder pads that protect the upper body with one that covers most of the chest and padding down the back. The front and back parts meet under the armpits, but there is also a slight gap towards the outer part of the ribcage. His stick penetrated this gap and went directly into my ribs, proceeding to smash every cubic millimetre of air from my lungs in one fell swoop.

I had been "winded" many times on a rugby field, but this took things to a new level. It felt like a vacuum was going to cause my lungs to contract resulting in the collapse of my ribcage. But the most frightening part of this type of incident is the seemingly unbearable task of trying to suck air in because no matter how hard you try, it seems impossible to take a breath.

I collapsed to my knees, and knew I was going to end up curled into a foetal position on the ice, but just before my head descended to ground zero, I turned to my left to see my attacker laughing loudly as he skated away and made sure to note that he had a large white number six on the back of his red team jersey.

This would not be forgotten.

The game continued, which suggested that neither of the officials on the ice had seen the incident, but most of my teammates sitting on the bench were indeed aware of what had just happened and were shouting out in anger—not that anything would happen as a result.

After what felt like several hours, but was likely only a few seconds, I managed to squeeze enough air into my lungs to be able to get to my feet and slowly grovel back to the bench. My teammates asked if I was okay, and I spent the remainder of the first period with my head between my knees as my breathing returned to something like normal. As the whistle went for halftime (we played two periods of twenty minutes), our coach checked on my condition and as I was feeling a bit better, I said I was okay to play again.

The second period got under way, and although it became clear that the top two lines were getting a lot more ice time than the third and fourth, I did manage to get out there for a few shifts, during which I tried to contribute without getting in any of my teammates' way (a task that was a lot harder than it sounded if you are not very good at stopping, or turning left or right, or skating backwards). Unfortunately, we were getting a bit of a drubbing, and as we approached the end of the game, were trailing by something like

6-1. With the game pretty much gone, and nothing much to lose, the coach decided to allow the third and fourth lines more ice time, and with only a minute left on the clock I was over the boards for the last time on my hockey debut.

Play was going back and forth but the puck was soon in the corner behind our opposition's goal (for the pedants amongst us, they aren't really "corners" as the rink is oval in shape—but you know what I mean) and it was being protected by one of the other team's players, who was facing the glass and boards with his back to the rest of the ice, meaning the number on the back of his jersey was clearly visible.

It was a large white number six.

Now, as mentioned before, part of professional hockey includes "checking," where one player smashes into another player to stop them progressing up the ice or to knock them off possession of the puck. Checking is supposed to involve body-to-body contact with the stick being held out of the way in one hand.

This is NOT allowed in a 'Safe' Hockey League.

Another technique known as "cross-checking" is where a player smashes into another player—usually from behind so they don't know you're coming—while holding their stick in front of them across their chest, with their hands around a metre apart. This ensures the opposition player feels the full force of the "hit" through the combination of a solidly held stick and the weight of the other player's body.

This is a very dangerous manoeuvre that can badly injure someone, and it is *not* allowed in a 'Safe' Hockey League (obviously); it is also seen as a heinous crime in professional hockey leagues.

Retribution: A Dish Best Served on Ice

It is worth considering, at this time, the various options for head and facial protection in a 'Safe' Hockey League. Helmets were compulsory on the ice, but the choice of face coverings were down to individual preference. The majority of amateur players will use a "cage" that attaches to the helmet, fastens under the chin, and protects the face from stray sticks, elbows, hands and the puck, which, as a very hard piece of rubber, when travelling very fast is a pretty dangerous object.

Most professional players will wear a clear plastic visor over their eyes and upper face so they can see everything on the ice (this also helps with them being recognized on television for those very lucrative image rights contracts). But some players, professional and amateur, will take the bravado/ego/stupid approach, and try to convince everyone they are tougher than teak, and not wear anything over their faces.

As someone who had broken his nose several times playing rugby, which often resulted in some form of surgery to straighten my nose and remove bits of bone from my nasal passage, and who was also still creating an income stream as a professional musician, I had opted for the cage (a fast-travelling puck hitting you in the face has a very good chance of separating you from your front teeth, not good for a musician's embouchure).

Number Six fitted into the bravado/ego/stupid category by trying to demonstrate he was too tough for face protection. At this point he was still in the corner with his back to the rest of the ice. The puck was between his skates whilst he was pushing left and right against two of my teammates and trying to "run the clock down" by not letting them get to it. I, having not managed to keep up with play very well, was around two-thirds of the length of the ice away, but the opportunity now in place flicked a switch in my psyche.

Although not a very good skater, I could actually go in one direction fairly rapidly—it was the turning and stopping that were the problems, neither of which I was going to need in order to execute on the plan that had formed in my mind—and so I set off towards the corner where play was currently based. I pushed hard on my skates, drove my legs like an Olympic speed skater, pumped my arms as we had been taught in our beginner's course, and, with ever increasing pace, hurtled across the ice. My target was very simple and very clear: it was a large white number "6" on the back of a red hockey jersey, and with around three metres to go, I pulled my stick up into both hands, held it out in front of me and, smash, hit the bastard at full speed just below the shoulder blades.

The initial impact caused his torso to hit the boards and glass and his head to jerk backwards, but such was the force with which he was hit, his head followed his body and his face catapulted into the glass with a sound rather like a clap of thunder, resulting in his nose, and other parts of his face, appearing to explode in a shower of blood. This was followed by a short period of total silence, rather like when you see a small child fall over while running: they are quiet until they realize what just happened and the wailing starts.

But what happened next was quite interesting.

Number Six then complied with the laws of gravity by slowly sliding downwards with his face against the glass. This caused his (unprotected) chin to bounce off the ledge on the top of the boards with a dull thud, before finishing the slide completely unconscious face down on the ice in an ever-widening pool of blood. It struck me later that if this had been a Tom and Jerry Cartoon, the slide would have been accompanied by a descending glissando from a bunch of discordant violins as part of the soundtrack.

In his wake, he had left a deposit of blood and other bodily fluids on the glass and boards that looked like someone had turned up with a large paintbrush and tin of red paint and decided to randomly daub a strip from around the six-foot mark to the ice.

But what then?

For a few seconds, no one moved, but most team sports are tribal in nature, and male ego usually results in some form of retribution if a teammate has been taken out by an opponent, and I quickly became the focus of attention from the rest of Number Six's side. There was a lot of swearing, and punching, and grappling, and whacking of sticks, all in my direction, but soon my own teammates joined in and what resulted was a mass brawl that not only involved everyone on the ice, but also cleared everyone off the benches.

I found out later that both officials had never seen anything like it and didn't quite know what to do, but they began blowing their whistles loudly while shouting at us all to stop, which didn't really have much impact, because the violence only really slowed down once we were too knackered to carry on whacking each other. Once the last of the other team's players was dragged off me, I managed to get to my feet to see that Number Six was now awake and sitting up with his back to the boards. His face was a bit of a mess, and he was sitting in a pool of his own blood, which looked highly vibrant against the white of the ice. One of the officials took me by the arm and led me to the tunnel off the ice, telling me I was banned for the rest of the game (which only turned out to be around twenty seconds of play).

Well, He Started It

Once back in the locker room I sat on a bench and felt a mixture of emotions. While I was glad to have got my own back for the cheap shot I took at the start of the game, I knew it was a pretty childish thing to do—but, then again, *he* had started it.

Was what he did "cheating?"

Well, it was against the rules of the game no matter what level you played at, so I would say yes.

What was his aim?

Clearly to take one of the opposition players out of the game and so give his team an advantage (although my team probably played better without me than with me), as well as to feed his Neanderthal ego.

Within a few minutes the rest of my team were back off the ice and greeted me with a mixture of astonishment and praise.

"Holy shit Paul—WHAT a hit!"

"That got the bastard back, eh? Brilliant."

"Don't mess with the Brit!"

"Rule Britannia—good one, Paul."

Then our coach came in.

"That guy is an asshole. He can be a pretty good player but rather than be in a team in a higher division, he keeps playing down here with people so he can bully them. Well done, Paul—he deserved that."

Once showered and changed, I headed back to my car to drive home. As I left the arena, a couple of the opposition players saw me and walked over. I was a bit wary they might start something, but instead they shook my hand and told me Number Six was the "ultimate dickhead" who they never wanted on their team in the first place. They had seen what he did to me and were banning him from playing with them again… although the injuries he sustained that night would keep him out for a while anyway.

And what was the ultimate aftermath?

I got an email two days later telling me that as a result of my actions in the first game, I was being handed a ten-game ban from the league, which, to the best of my knowledge, is still the longest in the league's history. This meant I only had one game of the season left, and as the team went on to play well without me, I turned up to watch and have a beer rather than play again. I was in a fair amount of pain myself for a few days after that first game, and an X-ray revealed three cracked ribs. When I explained the incident to my doctor, she said I was lucky I didn't puncture a lung.

Like I said, "safe hockey" can be a bit of an oxymoron.

But when it comes to running up the hill called sporting cheats, where do Boston Qualifiers, bib mules, dopers and hockey thugs align? Well, they are all trying to get ahead of the opposition through nefarious means, and although I can't do much about those Mexican runners, or professional dopers, in retrospect, I'm glad I didn't let Number Six get away with it.

CHAPTER 7

A Hill Called Alzheimer's

I walked into the empty bathroom to see the hot water tap was running and the toilet hadn't been flushed.

I walked into the empty kitchen and saw that two burners on the stove were on full, blazing hot and glowing red.

An hour or so later I sat down for my dinner and my mum put a plate of food in front me consisting of cold meats, two fried eggs and oven chips (fries). The eggs were cooked but the chips were still mostly frozen.

As I walked up the steep stairs to my room in the converted attic, I began to see things I had never seen in the thirty-five years I had been visiting my parents' home: cobwebs and dust.

It was September 2019, and my mum and dad were eighty-eight and eighty-nine years old. Little did I know that because of the COVID-19 pandemic, it was the last time I would see them in person for exactly two years.

But what I had seen in the bathroom, kitchen, and other areas of the house bothered me.

Why? Are those things really an issue?

Well, if you had ever met my parents, you would know that these conditions were as much out of character as you could possibly get. Their house was like a shrine to domestic organization, hygiene and cleanliness. My mum's cooking could put any half-decent Michelin chef to shame, maybe not in the cordon bleu category, but certainly in the quality of the recipes she cooked. My mum was "sharp as a tack." Her no-nonsense approach to everything in life led her to be one of the most organized, disciplined and structured people in the history of humanity (I come by it honestly!). But seeing this decline in the image I had had of her my whole life led me to think that at eighty-eight, age was really starting to catch up with her.

As well as being so efficient and well-organized, my parents were both very proud people who, despite their increasing age, were still doing all their own housekeeping, grocery shopping, gardening, laundry and cleaning. Their independence was a vital part of their existence. Any previous attempts I had made to carefully suggest they may need to consider outside help for the upkeep of the house had been met with scoffs and rolling of eyes. They were *"perfectly capable of looking after ourselves, thank you very much."* But this was different. I had never seen taps left running, unflushed toilets or uncooked food, and the unattended glowing burners were a major safety hazard.

I left the UK the following day to head back to Canada and spent most of my journey pondering what I had witnessed. I drafted an email outlining my observations. Then I drafted it again. Then I deleted it rather than appear to offend them. Then I drafted it again—and again—and again. I outlined some facts: the toilet had not been flushed, the tap had been left running, burners on the stove had been left on, the chips weren't cooked. I rewrote it repeatedly. Did it make the point? Was it too aggressive? What would their reaction be?

I was also concerned these observations were just the tip of the iceberg: leaving the cooker on was bloody dangerous. Eating undercooked food was not healthy, especially for people of their age, although my dad would rarely eat anything if it wasn't so hot it was still effectively cooking on the plate. I knew that if I didn't say anything and at a later date these issues came back to cause a major incident, I would have to live with it on my conscience.

So, I re-drafted the letter again. And again.

I finally settled on a version that I thought read as both a positive and well-meaning reinforcement of how well they were doing at their age, but also indicated that I was becoming a little concerned at some of the things I had seen the last time I had been there. Well, I *thought* it was positive and well-meaning.

Apparently not, as it didn't go down well, although it did at least inspire my parents to hire a lady in the village to come and clean each week for them. But the most important point I had been trying (and clearly failing) to make, was that I was concerned that my parents' age was starting to impact their living and maybe it was time they considered some help.

Our weekly FaceTime video calls were put to good use to smooth things over and try to assuage their disgruntlement at being "judged" like that. And I introduced the concept that it might be a good idea to consider moving to a smaller and more manageable house. My dad was open to this, but my mum was having none of it.

"The last time I leave this house will be feet first in a box," she would say after any attempt to convince her to consider moving.

But over the weeks and months of weekly calls, I started to see a gradual decline in my mum's cognitive reasoning as well as a reduced ability to communicate… to the point where if I was to mention anything that contradicted one of her strongly held beliefs, she barely reacted, and certainly didn't give the forceful response I had come to expect of her.

By the early spring of 2020 we were deep into the pandemic, and its accompanying lockdowns and flight restrictions meant it was unlikely I would be travelling back to the UK anytime soon. But what set my alarm bells ringing like a fire engine on steroids was something my dad said on one Sunday-morning call. I asked him what they were having for Sunday lunch (the most important and carefully planned meal of the week in our family).

"I'm cooking a nice piece of beef in the slow cooker," my dad replied.

Hold on—what did he say?!

"I said I'm cooking a nice piece of beef in the slow cooker. I've put onions, carrots, parsnips and some celery in. We are having new potatoes and runner beans as well."

"Did you say *you* were cooking it?"

"Yes."

"Since when did you cook Sunday lunch, or *any* meal for that matter?"

At this point my parents had been married for sixty-seven years, and apart from things like beans on toast, or a bowl of soup, my dad had never really cooked anything—mostly because the kitchen was my mum's domain.

"It's just easier that way," he replied, with no response from my mum.

The next morning, I called my parents' family doctor and spoke to the community nurse. She promised to reach out to them, and over the course of the next few weeks she started the process of getting social workers involved and generating a full assessment of my parents' status. Her reports back to me revealed that my mum was suffering from dementia and that the Dementia Rapid Response team were being dispatched to visit and do a more thorough investigation into her condition. Occupational therapists were also included in the process, and I have to say the organization and support offered to my parents by the National Health Service, Social Services and the local authority in the UK were very helpful and active.

However, the visits to check on my mum usually involved a sit down and chat with a cup of tea and a biscuit or a sandwich which of course my dad had to prepare and clean up after. He was having to deal with mum's worsening condition as well as host daily visitors, creating more work and stress.

It Was a Long Two Years

By September 2021, exactly two years after my last visit, travel was opening to the point I could finally return to the UK and get to be with my parents again for a couple of weeks. I thought I had a rough idea of what to expect, but I was way short of the mark. Whilst my dad was doing everything he could to provide the care my mum needed, it was very clear that as he was now ninety-one-years-old, there were clear limits to what this could include. I was shocked that Social Services had not recommended my mum should go into care, but they were only at my parents' house for a couple of hours each afternoon, during which my mum would sit and chat with them.

"Mrs. Weston is doing okay, and her husband appears able to cope," were typical update reports.

How wrong they were, because what I was quickly going to discover while I was there, was that my mum had now developed serious incontinence issues that required a bedding change several times each night, and as the primary caregiver, my dad was up constantly having to tend to her. If my dad was having a quiet nap on the sofa in the afternoon (which he needed after being up for most of the night), mum would head out of the house into the village on her own, where she would be found wandering around by someone and brought back to the house. During shopping trips to get groceries, my dad would lead with a list while mum was supposed to stay with the shopping cart, but even while I was there helping, when I turned my back she would wander off to the point we had to get the shop to go on a "search and rescue mission," only to find her trying to get out of the ladies' toilet.

It was not dissimilar to trying to control an inquisitive toddler.

She would decide to lay the kitchen table for breakfast constantly throughout the day. Then clear it away and wash all the unused dishes. Then lay it again, and clear it away again, time after time. This was starting to drive my dad, not a naturally patient man, up the wall.

My mum never had any interest in cycling, but one afternoon she sat down, picked up a cycling magazine I had brought with me, and read it out loud from cover to cover.

One day my car keys went missing, resulting in a rather stressful search for them. They were in the garbage can.

If left unattended, she was known to go up to a bedroom and empty all the contents of a wardrobe onto the bed then tell me she didn't have any clothes to wear.

She was also starting to get very aggressive with us both. When it was time to go to bed she would refuse to leave her chair, and even if we did get her up, she would refuse to go up the stairs and would physically push back against us. My dad told me she had tried pushing chairs into him, and he had hidden the cooking knives; he had also hidden the house key, so she couldn't leave the house—which made her even more angry.

This was not my mother.

This was someone so badly affected by dementia that I was starting to lose any recognition of her.

I took the opportunity to meet with and discuss my mother's case with the Dementia Team and it was decided that a more thorough assessment was required. A psychiatrist was identified, and an assessment and report put in place. A few weeks later, the report was emailed to me.

My mother was diagnosed with Alzheimer's disease.

The diagnosis fitted well with what I had seen with my own eyes. It also encouraged me to do my own research into something I had heard of in other people, but when it involves your own mother, you suddenly take things a lot more seriously.

Alzheimer's is a neurodegenerative disease that usually starts slowly but progressively worsens and it is the cause of 60–70% of cases of dementia. As of 2020, there were approximately fifty million people worldwide with Alzheimer's disease. The most common early symptom is difficulty remembering recent events, but as the disease advances, symptoms can include problems with language, disorientation (including easily getting lost), mood swings, loss of motivation, self-neglect and behavioral issues. As a person's condition declines, they often withdraw from family and society. Gradually, bodily functions are lost, ultimately leading to death.

The cause of Alzheimer's disease is poorly understood. There are many environmental and genetic risk factors associated with its development, and no treatments can stop or reverse its progression, though some may temporarily improve symptoms. A healthy diet, physical activity, and social engagement are generally beneficial in aging and may help in reducing the risk of cognitive decline and Alzheimer's. It most often begins in people over sixty-five years of age, although up to ten percent of cases are early-onset impacting those in their thirties to mid-sixties and it affects about six percent of people sixty-five years and older—women more often than men.

Alzheimer's generally unfolds in three stages—early or mild, middle or moderate and late or severe—and people with the diagnosis experience a progressive pattern of cognitive and functional impairment. The disease is known to target the hippocampus which is associated with memory, and this is responsible for the first symptoms of memory impairment. As the disease progresses, so does the degree of memory impairment.

After doing my own research, I felt I could have made my own diagnosis, so clear were my mum's symptoms, but what next? It was clear that my dad could only cope for so long on his own, and that a care home was going to have to be the solution, despite my mum, during times when she was relatively lucid, refusing to entertain the idea ("the last time I leave this house…").

Even though the solution was logical, my dad was very reluctant and wanted to "do his job as a dutiful husband" and be there for her as long as he could. When I think back to those very difficult times, I realize it was then my dad became my number one hero for what he did for my mum. His resolute determination to be there for her, to be her support and ultimate rock in life showed me the depths of the love he had for her. This was his ultimate hill, and nothing was going to stop him climbing it for my mum.

But alas, it eventually became too much for him and by October 2022, she was found a place in a very comfortable location that provided residential, medical and dementia care, but for a princely sum. Just prior to this placement I had spent some time with my parents on what was to be the final time I would see my mother at home. It had been a difficult time trying to help my dad cope, get as much help from the authorities as I could, and spend time with mum during the ever-shorter periods when she knew who I was. She was becoming very flustered and frustrated with not being able to understand what was happening and on the day I was due to leave, she was sitting at the kitchen table wiping the table mats after another meal that hadn't taken place.

I sat next to her, and she looked at me.

I held her hand and told her I had to leave to go home.

"Okay," she replied, "when will you be back?"

"In a few weeks I will come over and see you again," I said, knowing that by then she would likely not recognize me.

"Paul," she said looking into my eyes, "I just need to know that you love me."

"Of course I love you."

She smiled, patted my hand and said, "Well, that's all that really matters then."

I think she knew at that moment that her ability to communicate with her only child had come to an end.

There then began my own journey towards a better understanding of this terrible disease and the implications not only on patients but those close to them. I learned that Alzheimer's is very often a hereditary illness, and I was fortunate to be able to get involved in an assessment process that could identify early onset dementia. This started with a thirty-minute live memory test, which got me a little worried because at one point I couldn't for the life of me remember five words I had been given about ten minutes previously. But apparently, I did okay, and was told the bits I forgot were typical for a "man of my age" (isn't that a bit 'ageist'?). Further testing went on to reveal I was doing okay and my chances of suffering from any form of dementia were very low.

My visits to the UK were now a lot more frequent in order to support my dad, who although now living alone, was entering a completely new chapter of his life as he was doing all his own cooking and showing skills even he didn't realize he had. New recipes and instructions were being dug up on YouTube on his iPad, and he was particularly proud of being able to make pancakes, fry an egg and cook a steak (to perfection), as well as expand on his slow-cooker recipes. And never once did he *ever* complain about having to survive on his own (although in fairness, he would complain about pretty much everything else… politics, the state of the roads, the England football team, commercials on TV…).

She Was Right Though

My dad generally visited my mum about three times a week, but I was only able to get there approximately every three months, and the continued decline in my mum's condition was quite alarming. But I was determined do something in support of what was such a sad outcome for our family and managed to secure a charity spot at the 2023 London Marathon (despite stating I would never run a marathon again) in support of Alzheimer's Research. This was close to my sixtieth birthday, and I set up a 60@60 fundraising event that saw me run 60 miles in seventeen hours which, along with my London Marathon efforts, raised over $8,000.

I had been doing a major fundraising event every year for quite some time and had a loyal following of people who were all very generous in their donations. But this time it was a little different, as Alzheimer's was a subject very close to many people's hearts. I learned that a close musical friend's husband, recently retired at the age of sixty-five from a very highly paid position with a great pension plan, had expected they were set up for many very happy years of travel to a number of properties they owned while enjoying the house they had been building. He was diagnosed with Alzheimer's and within six months had declined so much he did not recognize any member of his family. My friend was coming to terms with the fact her life was now transformed into being a carer for what could be twenty years.

I learned that a former colleague's wife was diagnosed in her mid-fifties, and he spent the next few years looking after her—during which time she got to the stage she did not know who he, or anyone else, was. She passed away five years later and his statement that "we lost her twice" was a harsh declaration of the impact the disease can have on a family.

Another former colleague shared that his father, whom I had met several years previously, had also spent the final few years of his life in a home dealing with Alzheimer's before passing away.

Other harrowing stories included one of a lady who nursed her mother for more than thirty years, only to be diagnosed herself in her late fifties. Determined not to force her daughter to go through what she had experienced as a carer, which she felt had ultimately ruined her life, she elected to travel to Switzerland where she could legally opt for euthanasia.

As my mum was not able to recognize anyone around her, particularly my dad and me, she slipped into her own world. She was comfortable in her bed and my visits revolved around listening to her chat away to herself about nothing in particular. On some occasions she would burst into song and give me a rendition of some chorus she had sung with her choir many years previously. She would look at me then shout that "she wasn't going to have any of it anymore—oh no!"

On one lovely summer afternoon, she told me there had been a man looking in the window at her and shook her head and "tutted" very loudly. As I was leaving the home I dropped into the office to talk to the home manager and mentioned that she was likely hallucinating about the man looking in at her, only to discover the window cleaners had been working that morning.

After ten months in her home, my mum was assessed as within the final three months of her life and placed in palliative care. My transatlantic journeys became more frequent, and at the time of writing, it is over a year later and she is still going—which is typical of her: she just has to prove everyone wrong.

Alas, some hills we run up out of choice.

Some hills we run up as a challenge.

Some hills are optional.

Some hills are compulsory.

Running Up Hills

Sometimes we have to watch other people run up hills, and Alzheimer's is one of those hills we have to attempt as part of a journey on our own as caretakers and loved ones, of those suffering with the disease.

But those making the most challenging ascent are those afflicted.

If only they were aware of it—or maybe not.

Ultimately the hill called Alzheimer's is tough for everyone.

CHAPTER 8

A Hill Called Tourette

"STOP THAT!" shouted my teacher, "You are distracting everyone. If you can't control yourself, you will be sent to the headmaster."

I was eight years old.

"Paul Weston, stop making those silly faces, you are annoying me," said my teacher.

I was nine years old.

"What's the matter with you? Are you faulty or something? Why do you keep pulling those faces?" asked my teacher.

I was ten years old.

"Are you broken or something? Why do you keep trying to crack your jaw? You'll hurt yourself. Stop it," said my teacher.

I was eleven years old.

"Weston! Stop making those ridiculous faces—are you defective or something?" said my teacher.

I was twelve years old.

"Wow, you must be really damaged if you can't stop twitching like that," said my teacher.

I was thirteen years old.

"Hey everyone, look at Weston, he's having a twitching fit again," said my teacher. The class all looked at me and laughed. I was fourteen years old.

"You will never make anything of your life if you can't control those tics," said my teacher.

I was fifteen years old.

Faulty.

Broken.

Defective.

Damaged.

By the time I was sixteen, the message was clear—I wasn't like everyone else. I had a problem.

Many young people display "habits" as they grow up. Raising of eyebrows, stretching open their mouths, shaking their heads, constant blinking. I was no different, and when I was around seven years old my parents took me to the family doctor who told them I would "probably grow out of it."

Well, I didn't.

Instead, I tried to suppress what I believed was a "tic disorder" or "nervous twitch." Suppressing the urge not to tic when your body is demanding it is really hard. It is like holding your eyes open for as long as you can. There is no logical reason why you shouldn't be able to keep them open forever. Your eyelids aren't "heavy," so it's not like holding a weight at arm's length. Unless there are a lot of foreign objects floating around, there is no need to close them. But you just want to close them. There is an urge to close them. You can only fight it for so long, until you give in, close them, and likely feel a surge of relief run through your body.

That is what it is like when you have a tic disorder. You know you should be able to control your tics. There is no reason why you can't stop shaking your head, or rolling your eyes, or raising your eyebrows, or flexing your shoulders, or clicking your jaw bone, or sniffing loudly, or clearing your throat when there is nothing there, or opening and closing a fist, or tapping your knuckles on a desk, or raising your heel off the ground over and over and over, or grinding your teeth to the point your jaw and mouth ache, or keep twisting your head to one side so that your neck hurts so bad you just want to rip your head off… and so on and so on.

I left school, and home, and joined the Royal Marines Band Service at the age of sixteen. Even though I was starting out on a career as a military musician, I had to pass Basic Training: the act of being turned from a civilian to a member of the military.

We had to learn about personal hygiene, how to clean our accommodation, do our laundry and clean and maintain our uniforms. There was physical training, equipment and weapons training and we had to learn how to shoot. We also had to acquire field craft including basic survival, map reading and the fundamentals of tactical soldering.

But of course, the key aspect of initial military life was drill.

This involved being part of a sixty-man troop of fellow "new entries" learning to march in step, swing our arms in unison, turn left, right and about together, and of course, stand still for long periods of time. This was an education in self-discipline, and it filled me with dread. I desperately wanted to be a Royal Marines Musician but knew that if I did not pass basic training, my career would be over before it started. I had no problems with the physical training, or any other part of "basics," but drill kept me awake at night.

What if I got a tic attack while we were on parade? I was bound to be shouted at and maybe disciplined and discharged for being "faulty," or "broken," or "defective" or "damaged" like my teachers had kept telling me. Drill was part of our daily training program, so we were constantly on parade. It always started with an inspection, and with sixty young musicians in our troop, that meant standing still for a long time, either "at ease" (which doesn't mean you can move around, it just means your feet are slightly apart and your arms are behind your back) or to "attention," where any form of moving was forbidden.

I managed to get through the first week without getting noticed, but at some point after that I remember we had to stand at attention for quite a long time and I was really fighting off the urge to tic. My head wanted to shake, and I wanted to crack my jaw and roll my shoulders. The temptation finally got the better of me (it always did at some point), and I quickly shook my head.

It felt so good to quickly release that urge.

I thought I had got away with it, until our drill sergeant, a wonderful man called Tony Martin, looked over at me. He stopped inspecting the musician he was with for a moment, watched me a little longer, then resumed what he was doing.

Eventually he got to me.

"Good morning, Weston."

"Good morning, Sergeant."

He looked me up and down, pausing on my boots.

"Boots are coming along nicely."

"Yes, Sergeant."

"Make sure you clean the rest of the boot, don't just spit and polish the toecaps."

"Yes Sergeant."

"And Weston."

"Sergeant?"

"Breathing… always keep breathing… deep breaths… that will help you."

"Yes, Sergeant."

And with that, he moved to inspect the next junior musician.

There was a clear message there. It was like he understood me, like he knew there was something going on, that he had seen it before, and most importantly, that he wanted to help.

When you join the military, your Drill Instructor takes the place of your parents. There is a common misconception that the first thing they say to you when you are on parade for the first time is, "right then, I'm mother and your father now."

I never heard Sergeant Martin say those words, but he played that part. His job was to "break us in," but he did it with a calm assurance and understanding.

He was a Royal Marines Commando, an elite soldier, and we were Royal Marines Musicians. Same uniform, same cap badge, and while we were required to undertake many military roles in conflict zones around the world, we were not front-line infantry soldiers like the Commandos were. But Tony Martin "got" us. He understood that we couldn't be treated like Commando recruits, because that wouldn't have worked. Yes, he had a job, and we had to meet standards of discipline, of military "bearing". We had to display character and integrity and become part of the Royal Marines family so that we could be relied upon to be important members of the team. There were occasions when he shouted at us for not reaching a certain standard. He punished us with whole troop extra parades if someone's kit was below standard. He would keep us up very late for extra accommodation inspections, and while some of the disciplinary procedures were probably not justified, it was all part of the game to see how we reacted under pressure.

He was a fair man, and we all respected him one hundred percent.

Towards the end of our eight weeks of basic training, we had to attend personal interviews with both our Troop Officer, Lieutenant Paddy Quinlan, and Sergeant Martin. We didn't see our Troop Officer as much as the Troop Sergeant, but he was always on the periphery of what we were doing, keeping an eye on things. My interview started with the question of how I thought things were going, and I answered that I thought I was doing okay, I supposed. I didn't want to say I thought I was doing amazingly well—which I didn't, but figured being humble might be the best approach.

I was told I was indeed doing okay, that I was capable of doing everything that was thrown at me, but maybe I needed to come out of my shell a little more and display higher levels of confidence. This seemed fair comment as I was used to taking a backseat for anything new to me.

Then Lieutenant Quinlan brought up something I was dreading.

"Weston, we have noticed you appear to have something of a nervous twitch."

My heart sank, then started racing hard at what seemed like two hundred beats to the minute. This was it; this was where they were going to tell me I was done; my military career was over.

"Yes, Sir."

"Do you know you are doing it?"

"Yes, Sir, but I can't do anything to stop it."

"Well, you probably can't, but maybe what you *can* do is control *when* you do it. Would that be possible?"

"I honestly don't know, Sir."

"Sergeant Martin tells me you hardly ever do it on parade, and the PT (Physical Training) staff haven't said anything to us when you are in the gym with them, so they haven't noticed, or they would certainly say something.

"We have seen it in you when you are doing general work like cleaning your kit or the accommodation," he continued. "Is that when it happens the most?"

"There don't seem to be specific times when it appears, it often seems random," I replied.

"Weston, do you get nervous?" asked Sergeant Martin.

"Sometimes Sergeant, it depends on what I am doing."

"Is there anything you have done in Basic Training that has made you nervous?"

"Probably going on parade knowing my tic was likely to get me into trouble."

"And has it?"

"No, Sergeant."

"Well, I have honestly only noticed it on parade once," he said, "and what did I tell you?"

"Keep taking deep breaths."

"Yes—I think your breathing could really help you."

Lieutenant Quinlan then added, "We don't think this is an issue, so long as you don't start twitching at important times. It is something you are going to have to work on, and you will be the at the centre of people's jokes and piss-taking at times, but everyone gets that for something they do, so it will be a test of your character to rise above it and show them you can succeed in your career. Do you think you can do that?"

"I'll try, Sir."

"Good man."

And for the first time in my life, I felt validated and accepted for who I was. Maybe if my schoolteachers had taken that type of approach I wouldn't have suffered as much as a boy. I left that interview with renewed confidence in the knowledge that if I could work on my tic disorder and control it whenever I could, I could succeed in my career.

I went on to win the award for Best All-Round Musician on completion of training and was the only member of my New Entry Troop that went on to secure a commission to Officer. I stayed in the Royal Marines Band Service for twenty-six wonderful years. My life as a military musician required me to stand still on important parades for many, many hours, often on live television at major events that were broadcast around the world. I spent several years serving onboard the Royal Yacht *BRITANNIA* providing musical support to all members of the British Royal Family, and I travelled around the world entertaining the Heads of State of dozens of countries. All these activities challenged my ability to control my tic disorder, and although there were times when it was a bit touch-and-go, I don't believe it ever once affected my work.

You Can If You Really Want To

Later in my career when I was assessed for Officer Selection, I had to undergo an intense process of tests (physical and mental), interviews, exams and presentations, at which I was successful and I went on to become a Director of Music, requiring me to take charge of large groups of musicians, often performing in some of the world's greatest venues. I got to meet and be in the presence of many VIPs and, again, I had to carefully control my tics to avoid drawing attention to them when it really mattered. I reached the second highest rank possible in my branch before retiring from the military, after which I emigrated to Canada and started my own consultancy focusing on business and leadership development.

This led to a lot of opportunities to deliver training classes as well as many key-note speeches and presentations, often to thousands of delegates at a time at some major international events. And, again, this required me to continue to control my tic disorder in a way that did not draw attention to it and allowed me to deliver my content with confidence and professionalism.

Looking back, I was very lucky to have received the advice and acceptance I did during my basic training. If I had only listened to my teachers, I believe my life would have been very different. But despite having a very successful military and business career, taking control of my tics always took a lot of strength and willpower. If I was standing on parade for any length of time, the urge to shake my head, blink forcefully, roll my shoulder or crack my jaw became almost irresistible, but I developed a number of techniques to release the pressure in other ways. I would force my right big toe down really hard in my boot, then my left. I would clench my quadriceps (muscles above the knee) or suck my stomach in. I would tense my biceps or keep clenching my fists. All of these techniques allowed a small amount of relief that held me over until I could be alone for a fraction of a second, which is when I would enjoy a tic bonanza to release it all. This might be in my car on the way home. It may be in a cubicle in a toilet, or just behind a building in a quiet space. So long as it was somewhere I wouldn't get seen, I was going to be okay.

This carried forward into other aspects of my life. As a musician I occasionally got to stand in front of a band or orchestra to play a solo. This, of course, added more pressure than just being a member of the larger ensemble, and while it raised the levels of stress somewhat, I was again able to control things by breathing, or maybe clenching some unseen muscles in my body until I could grab a quiet moment to "release" everything. But what was interesting about music, was that once I started playing, I never felt the urge to tic. Once into the piece of music I was performing or rehearsing, my tics were never an issue. Indeed, some close friends, who were fully aware of my tic issue, often commented that they never noticed it when I was playing an instrument.

In my work as a professional speaker, I followed similar techniques to maintain control of my tics when standing in front of large groups of people at conferences or workshops, but I always needed the "escape" moment on completion. I was also very lucky to have some wonderful friends in my life who were there for me when things were tough, and my tics ran out of control. I remember on one occasion my band had finished playing a concert and as the Director of Music I was required to attend a post-concert reception with some VIPs. For some reason, my tics had been really bad that day and although I got through the concert (just about) I knew the reception was going to be a real challenge. But several of my Senior Non-Commissioned Officers came along with me (it may have been the free bar they were really there for) and two in particular stuck by my side in support by taking on some of the conversation and so ease some of the pressure from me (answering questions in a large social setting was often a trigger for my tics).

On another occasion, I was in my mid-twenties and playing in an important cup rugby match for my local club. There were several thousand spectators and as the team's Fly Half, I had a key role in the game. After about ten minutes, the pressure of the occasion was starting to have an effect on me and one of my tics (shaking my head very quickly being the "tic of the day") started to emerge in a manner I could not control. At a breakdown in play, my opposite number started to mock me. He shouted across how much of a fool I looked and started to copy my head shaking. This happened at every stoppage for about twenty minutes, until there was a passage of play when the ball was further up the field and the referee was looking in that direction. I heard a dull thud behind me that sounded like fist on face and turned around to see my opposite number lying unconscious on the ground.

"That told the bastard," said one of my very large teammates as he jogged past me.

While my basic training instructors ultimately supported and encouraged me, my tics were also a source of amusement and ridicule for some of my fellow junior musicians. But all this did was teach me how to develop a thicker skin, because no matter who you were at that age in the military, there would be something people would find about you they could use to make fun of you at your expense. It could be your skin colour. It could be your religion. It could be your accent. It could be where you came from. It could be some facial disfiguration. It could be your weight or appearance. It could be related to some part of the job you really struggled with. There really were no limits, but the worst thing you could do was react, because that just gave them more fuel for their taunting.

As my life went on, I started to put my feelings about the disadvantages of having tics into a box metaphorically marked "DO NOT OPEN," and carried on as best as I could. Some people tell you to try to suppress tics, like they are an urge such as smoking, or gambling, or drugs, that you can just stop if you try hard enough. I realized at an early age that it is not possible to suppress tics, so I focused on masking them.

When I had a little cough or throat clearing tic, which often happened when I was chatting with someone in a social group setting, I would put my hand over my mouth like I really had a bit of a cough going on.

When I had a blinking tic, I would wipe my eyes like I had something in them.

When my head shaking tic started up, I would look around as if a bug was flying near me.

And when I had a jaw cracking tic, I would rub my ear as if I had a blockage or something.

I doubt I fooled everyone but assumed most people "bought it" and I thought that I was "getting away with it." So, as I headed through my thirties, forties and fifties, my tics never stopped me from doing anything I wanted to do. Professionally I had built two successful careers, as a military officer and a business owner.

I went from being a professional military musician to a semi-professional civilian musician and continued to play to a reasonably high standard in some great ensembles. I went from being a senior military officer, to being a business owner in the C-Suite space with opportunities to speak at some major international events. I went from playing competitive sports such as rugby and cricket to becoming a successful Ironman triathlete as well as representing Canada at several Age Group Triathlon World Championships. And all the while seemingly pushing my tics to one side by masking them, hiding them, pretending they weren't there because I had developed some techniques to manage them.

You Can't Deny Everything Forever

But, in reality, all I was doing was living in denial.

I was trying to live without them, and led myself to believe they didn't exist and that most people in my life didn't really notice them. But this wasn't true because there were times when the issue of tics would appear as a topic of conversation when I was with a group of people, and it became very uncomfortable.

The classic British 1970s comedy series *Fawlty Towers* has an episode called "Gourmet Night" and in it special guests are invited for a black-tie dinner. Two of the guests were called Mr. and Mrs. Twitchen and another, a Colonel Hall, had a bad "twitch" that manifested itself as a vigorous shake of the head. Part of the ensuing "humour" was related to the confusion and irony of the names and characteristics of the cast, and as someone with a tic disorder, this episode always made me feel uncomfortable.

But by living in denial of my tic issue, it was quite a shock on one occasion in my thirties when I attended a gathering of friends for a British Comedy Night where we had some drinks and snacks while watching some famous British shows. After some *Monty Python* and *Black Adder*, we got to *Fawlty Towers*, and while we were debating which episode to watch, I overheard the host say, "Don't put 'Gourmet Night' on while Paul is still here."

And I thought no one had noticed.

On another occasion I was invited out to a comedy club to see some acts with friends, during which one of the "comedians" spent most of his act making fun of people with tics. My friends made a point of not laughing but were clearly very uncomfortable. When we left, they apologized to me.

And I thought no one had noticed.

On another occasion, I went to an antiques auction with some friends. I was the last one through the door of the building and trying to keep a low profile because I had a bit of a head tic going on that day. As we approached the desk to register, the man on reception looked at me and said "Woah, you don't want to come in here if you have a twitch mate—you'll end up bidding for a load of stuff you don't want!"

And I thought no one had noticed.

But although I felt like I could "mask" my tics, I recognized that my friends must be giving me a "free pass" by either accepting them or pretending not to notice, and life carried on… until early 2024.

It was a Wednesday lunchtime, and I was preparing some food in my kitchen. Although I was in Canada, I was listening to the "Drive" programme on the BBC Radio 5Live app on my phone. I liked the presenters as they usually delivered a nice blend of current affairs as well as some light-hearted topics of the day. Just after I logged on to listen, the subject matter changed to an "awareness day" for an important health issue, and I heard the words, "Tourette Syndrome." Now, while I was aware of this condition, I always assumed it manifested itself as an extreme form of tics that included whole body movements, as well as the uncontrollable urge to shout often obscene words out loud. This wasn't me of course: I just had a minor tic disorder. Tourette Syndrome was way more serious than that. But the presenter was interviewing someone from Tourette Action UK, as it was Tourette Awareness Day. She asked the interviewee about the symptoms of Tourette Syndrome.

The response changed my life in an instant.

"A person with Tourette Syndrome has at least two 'motor tics,' that is, they cannot control certain bodily movements, and at least one 'vocal tic,' which doesn't have to be shouting, it could be either a cough, clearing of the throat or a sniff."

Hang on…. what did she say?

I replayed the previous thirty seconds of the programme.

"A person with Tourette Syndrome has at least two 'motor tics,' that is, they cannot control certain bodily movements, and at least one 'vocal tic,' which doesn't have to be shouting, it could be either a cough, clearing of the throat or a sniff."

My world stopped.

I easily met the criteria.

I had Tourette Syndrome.

I stopped making my lunch and listened to the remainder of the interview. It was thoroughly enlightening in the explanation of how it impacted people. How children got bullied at school and how seriously it can affect their lives and upbringing.

They got that right.

The interview ended and I was immediately online to gather some facts:

What is Tourette Syndrome?[9]

Tourette Syndrome is a neurodevelopmental disorder that affects children, adolescents and adults. The condition is characterized by sudden, involuntary movements and/or sounds called tics.

Tics can range from mild/inconsequential to moderate and severe and are disabling in some cases.

Tourette Syndrome is one type of Tic Disorder. Tics are the primary symptoms of a group of childhood-onset neurological conditions known collectively as Tic Disorders and individually as Tourette Syndrome (TS), Persistent (Chronic) Motor or Vocal Tic Disorder and Provisional Tic Disorder. These three Tic Disorders are named based on the types of tics present (motor, vocal/phonic, or both) and by the length of time that the tics have been present.

---

[9] Source: The Tourette Association of America.

Symptoms

Motor Tics

Motor tics are movements. Simple motor tics include but are not limited to: eye blinking, facial grimacing, jaw move-ments, head bobbing/jerking, shoulder shrugging, neck stretching and arm jerking. Complex motor tics involve multiple muscle groups or combinations of movements and tend to be slower and more purposeful in appearance, (e.g., hopping, twirling, jumping).

Vocal/Phonic Tics

Vocal (phonic) tics produce a sound. Simple vocal tics include but are not limited to sniffing, throat clearing, grunting, hooting and shouting. Complex vocal tics are words or phrases that may or may not be recognizable but that consistently occur out of context. In 10-15% of cases, the words may be inappropriate (i.e., swear words, ethnic slurs, or other socially unacceptable words or phrases).

This type of vocal tic, called coprolalia, is often portrayed or mocked in the media as a common symptom of TS.

Onset of Tics and Duration

Tics typically emerge between the ages of 5 and 7 years, usually with a motor tic in the head or neck region. They tend to increase in frequency and severity between the ages of 8 and 12 years and can range from mild to severe. Most people with TS see improvements by late adolescence, with some becoming tic-free. A minority of people with TS continue to have persistent, severe tics into adulthood.

Tics can range from mild to severe and, in some cases, can be self-injurious and debilitating. Tics regularly change in type, frequency and severity—sometimes for reasons unknown and sometimes in response to specific internal and external factors, including stress, anxiety, excitement, fatigue and illness.

Prevalence

Tics occur in as many as 1 in 5 school-aged children at some time but may not persist. TS and other Tic Disorders combined are estimated to occur in more than 1 in 50 school-aged children in the United States. TS occurs in 1 in 160 (0.6%) school-aged children, although it is estimated that 50% are going undiagnosed. The reported prevalence for those who have been diagnosed with Tourette is lower than the true number, most likely because tics often go unrecognized. TS affects all races, ethnic groups and ages, but is 3-4 times more common in boys than in girls. There are no reliable prevalence estimates of TS and other Tic Disorders in adults. However, they are expected to be much lower than in children as tics tend to decline into late adolescence.

Causes

The causes of TS and other Tic Disorders remain unknown. These conditions tend to occur in families, and numerous studies have confirmed that genetics are involved. Environmental, developmental, or other factors may also contribute to these disorders but, at present, no specific agent or event has been identified. Researchers are continuing to search for the genes and other factors underlying the development of Tic Disorders.

My continued research went on to reveal that we "Touretters" get some "bonus" conditions often thrown in for good measure:

- *Attention Deficit/Hyperactivity Disorder (ADHD)*
- *Obsessive Compulsive Disorder or Behaviors (OCD/OCB)*
- *Behavioral or Conduct Issues*
- *Anxiety*

- *Learning Disability*
- *Social Skills Deficits and Social Functioning*
- *Sensory Processing Issues*
- *Sleep Disorders*

I could certainly relate to the tic components of TS, and indeed some of the co-occurring conditions felt familiar at the same time, notably OCD. Further research into the symptoms and implications of the condition led me to some organizations including Tourette Canada and the Tourette Association of America. Instantly I had found a family of people out there who shared what I had been living with all my life.

The next step was a formal diagnosis, which could only be completed by a neurologist, and as coincidence would have it, I already had an appointment in place in a couple of weeks' time due to a number of persistent headaches I had been dealing with for several years. At the appointment, it was quickly confirmed that I had Tourette Syndrome, which, due to the stress it often caused, was probably a contributing factor to my headaches. Things were starting to fall into place.

My return to the research also guided me to an interesting event due to take place a few weeks later in Dallas, Texas—"Tic-Con 24"—a convention for people with Tourette Syndrome, for which I quickly registered, and booked flights and lodging.

It was the most impactful weekend of my life.

At the age of sixty-one, I was talking to fellow "Touretters" for the first time ever. It was literally life-changing, as I got to share my experience and hear other people talk about theirs. There were support sessions for children who were growing up with the disorder and I got to speak to a lot of parents who were clearly concerned about the impact it would have on their children. I could tell them about the successes I had enjoyed in my life and how I had not let TS stop me doing anything I wanted to do.

There were educational guidelines for teachers (fifty years too late for me) and employers. There were notable celebrities there to talk about their lives and how TS had impacted them. There were people older than me who were able to share their lives and how they had kept moving on with TS. But one thing that leapt out at me was how strong Touretters were. It was like a superpower they were living with, because they had learned to become stronger, more determined, more disciplined and more resourceful in order to not only get through life, but also achieve all the things they wanted to achieve.

I did a lot of inward thinking about my own journey, and how I had got to where I had in life while living with TS. I was very lucky in that my condition was a lot less serious than many others I met at Tic-Con, and while I wasn't always successful, I could mask my tics for the most part. But more than anything, that weekend gave me the chance to release so much of me that I had kept locked away for so many decades.

The shame I felt.
The embarrassment.
The mocking.
The bullying.
The ignorant teachers.

And for the first time, I got to share an incident that I had NEVER shared with anyone EVER before, and which I now recognized as being part of my ultimate hill.

Growing up, I went to a comprehensive school (high school) in my hometown of Rotherham in South Yorkshire. Although that area of England was dominated by the steel and coal mining industries and was generally a typical working-class environment, my parents spent time lobbying the local education authority to get me into a school for which I was not in the catchment area but provided a music programme as part of their curriculum, which was very important to me. I had been making music for several years, and although there was a school orchestra and concert band, I was the only boy in my year who played either a violin or clarinet, which presented another set of challenges, because believe me, walking through the playground of a South Yorkshire comprehensive school in the morning carrying a violin took some courage.

One Monday afternoon, when I was thirteen, I had been attending a school orchestra rehearsal and was one of the last kids to leave the building. As I did not live in the same area as most of the others, I walked off on my own in a different direction, only to get ambushed by four of the senior school bullies.

They grabbed me hard.

"Okay twitcher—time to have some fun!"

They dragged me around the back of the school, ripped my violin and school bag off my shoulders, and hurled them into some bushes. My glasses were pulled off my face and thrown in the same general direction. Two of them then held me against the wall while another told me they were going to punch me every time I twitched. I stood as still as I could, but, as you might imagine, there was a certain amount of anxiety developing.

It started with a head tic.

Bang. A fist smashed into my stomach.

I tried to double over in order to protect myself and get some breath back.

"Come on Weston, give us some more."

One of them pulled my hair back so my head was raised.

Again, I tried to keep still.

My jaw jerked.

Bang. Another fist into my stomach.

I groaned and bent over, only to be pulled up straight again.

"Give us another Weston."

I kept still. Very still. There were four pairs of eyes burning into me.

My throat cough tic kicked in.

Bang. This was more to the side and into my ribcage, which still knocked the wind out of me.

I was pulled up again.

"Come on Weston—give us a new one!"

Still as I could be. Very, very still.

"Come on—twitch for us you wanker."

Blink.

Bang. Stomach again, this time I managed to free myself from their grip and ended up on my knees.

They gave me a couple seconds during which they had a good laugh before pulling me to my feet again.

"Come on Weston, give us some more."

Still. Very, very still.

Calm. Just their breathing to break the silence.

Eyebrows went up.

Bang. Ribcage again, but this time they let me fall to the ground so they could start with the kicking.

The boots started on my stomach, but as I curled up into a ball they rained in on my back and legs, then threw in a few downward stamps on my ribs and hips.

"You're a freakshow Weston, you should fuck off back to the nuthouse," the ringleader shouted, after which they decided they had had enough fun for one day and left my laying there.

I slowly got to my feet.

My stomach and ribs hurt, but at least my hands and face were okay. I imagine they didn't want there to be any clear signs they had beaten the shit out of me.

I found my glasses, violin and bag and headed home. Both my parents had fulltime jobs, so I was usually in the house first. This gave me time to get cleaned up and make sure they didn't notice what had happened to me.

I was embarrassed about my tic disorder and did not want to draw any attention to it. I knew that if I told my parents they would go straight to the school to make a complaint. The bullies would be identified and punished, which would then make me an even bigger target, and who knows what level of beating I would get next time. Better to just keep it all to myself—which I did for forty-eight years until I went to Tic-Con 24 and got to finally share it with my fellow Touretters.

This led to a lot of tears and a lot of hugging—they understood like no one else could understand.

It felt like I had found a new family.

MY people, and we are all running up the same hill.

CHAPTER 9

Getting to the Top

We all have hills in our lives.

For me they involve my own faffing, and the faffers who hold me up on a seemingly daily basis. Although I almost only ever travel with carry-on bags, there are times when I have no option but to check something (for example when I'm travelling to an international triathlon with my bike and other assorted equipment), and my history of lost luggage still makes me feel very uncomfortable.

The constant hassles related to the amount and type of packaging still make me shake my head in disbelief way more often than they should... if people would only see the light and wise up!

When all you want to do is get something done in an efficient and effective way, and yet you come across a jobsworth to stop the process cold. If only they could rid themselves of such a trait and change their outlook, they might actually find life more fulfilling (and do us all a favour).

Being indoctrinated into the passionate pursuit of a sporting team often feels like some form of child abuse that can infiltrate your mental well-being for life.

No matter how hard I try not to take sport seriously, I always fail. Why bother to almost break myself trying to qualify for a major sporting event or win something when I know I am likely to come second to someone who has bent every rule in the book to get there?

Good question, but I still push myself every year trying.

And when you think you have cracked pretty much everything life can throw at you, you have to watch your mother fall prey to dementia and Alzheimer's disease, and then realize just how helpless we really are at times.

My life has taken me to many places in the world and given me the chance to run up many hills. In a purely physical context, I have always managed to get to the top. But I have come to realize that there will always be hills in my life, some I have yet to encounter, and which may never be mastered, which will be a constant challenge for me. We could look at those hills and allow them to stop us. To believe they cannot be conquered. That they are for other people to run up while we take an easier route. Or we can take on the challenge of running up them. Of taking them on with strength, commitment and fortitude and not let them stop us from doing anything we want to do with our lives.

I also recognize now that all my life I had really been running up one constant hill, but it took sixty years before I could put a name to it. And this was a hill that made me stronger with each ascending step, because it was my *Touretter Superpower* that got me off the ground the day I got the shit kicked out of me at school, and which has driven me all my life towards being who I am. When I analyze what, over the years, would likely trigger my tics, they certainly include the areas we have discussed here.

My own faffing and that of others would get me going. As would the prospect that my luggage has been lost and futile attempts to overcome the challenges of packaging. The stresses of wanting my team to win something, or the continual frustration of seeing cheats prosper and, of course, the anxiety I felt watching my mum decline with dementia and ultimately Alzheimer's.

But I now realize that Tourette Syndrome really has helped make me who I am today because, despite what my teachers told me, I am not "faulty."

I am not "broken."

I am not "defective."

I am not "damaged."

Tourette Syndrome has given me a chance to be stronger and more determined to achieve what I have with my life.

As a "Touretter," almost everything I do has to be done with more strength and fortitude, and *that* is what has defined who I am, and not some incurable brain disorder. What an amazing group of people Touretters are: so strong, so brave, so determined, so understanding. It is an honour to have been welcomed onto their hill.

Once I had dodged the sheep urine heading in my direction, my run on that wet Derbyshire morning took me ever higher. The sheep were now up on the grassy banks looking down on me, rather like the crowd in a sporting stadium. I looked up and saw, through the gently swirling cloud, the metal cattle grid and rusty gate that signalled the pass's summit.

The final few steps took me to slightly flatter ground which allowed my breathing to calm and my heartbeat to slow. My hands touched down on the gate in order to signal success in having reached the top, and I turned around to look back down from where I had come.

Just then, the clouds cleared, and the sun broke through, illuminating the beautiful valley below.

That particular hill—like so many others we face in life—was a tough climb. But in mastering it I was rewarded with a spectacular view and the satisfaction of having found the resources within myself to do what many believe is impossible. It reminded me of the idea that, as a species, we are much more resilient than we realize. And, as individuals, we have extraordinary capabilities that can carry us through exceptional difficulties.

My wish for others isn't that they have no hills to run up (what fun would that be?) but, rather, that they make those climbs with determination, integrity and a terrifically good sense of humour.

It isn't easy.

But it's worth it.

Acknowledgments

I suppose when you write and publish a book about getting on with things rather than making excuses, you probably need to follow it up with another book shortly after.

Running in the Rain has been a greater success than I could ever have imagined, but getting something else down on paper has taken a bit longer than it should—but here we are at last.

Running Up Hills became a quite different project and while it may be construed as a bit of a moan, I hope it has been fun and a little poignant to get through.

A big thanks to my wonderful editor, Susan Crossman. Her attention to detail is so astute she is likely the only person I have ever met who could have given my mum a run for her money during her heyday.

Thanks also to Becky Norwood and her team at Spotlight Publishing House. They helped make *Running in the Rain* an International #1 Best Seller, so I am hoping for a repeat performance with this book.

I would have been short of content without all the people who have pissed me off over the years, so I suppose I should thank them—wherever they are.

As each chapter grew, I needed a pair of ears to listen while I tried out the flow and story-development, thank you Liisa Alton for not falling asleep and instead giving me the feedback I needed.

You think you have seen pretty much everything life has to offer by the time you reach sixty, but my introduction to the Tourette's community has been life changing. Thanks to all of them, but notably Jackie and Scott Nau, and Bret Holden for their friendship, support and inspiration.

At the time of writing, mum is still with us and is well looked after in her care home, and my dad and I continue to be grateful for the staff of Valley Lodge in Derbyshire for being there for her.

But the biggest thanks must go to the 'Old Fella'. He takes a bit of a hit through some of these pages, but as I have grown older, I have seen his unique qualities start to evolve into my own beliefs and habits. We both like a good moan, but the way he dealt with my mum's condition through her journey with Alzheimer's showed true love and devotion.

So, thanks for reading, and if you are still only 'page flicking', stop faffing around and buy it!

About Paul Weston

*P*aul Weston grew up in Yorkshire, England, and after a youth absorbed in music and sport, at age 16, joined the Royal Marines Band Service.

Over the next 26 years, his duties took him around the globe, and on completion of his military career, he immigrated to Canada where he joined the North American corporate world consulting in Leadership Development and Sales.

He also coach's executives, corporations and individuals in Time Freedom techniques, and is a sought-after keynote speaker.

A multiple Ironman and international triathlete, he is also an active classical musician as an orchestral instrumentalist and occasional soloist as well as guest conducting various ensembles across North America.

An established writer, his book, *Running in the Rain—Seriously… How Hard Can It Be?* became an International #1 Best Seller.

Paul lives in Newmarket, Ontario.

For more information on Paul and his work, please visit:

www.paulwestonconsulting.com
paul@paulwestonconsulting.com

Also by Paul Weston

Running in the Rain

A logical and systematic guide to being a better organized, functional, productive and committed person, in order to overcome your daily challenges and lead a truly fulfilling life.

Running in the Rain isn't hard—it's just a bit uncomfortable at times. But doesn't it feel good to know you stopped making excuses and just got out there and did it?

Life's the same. You can either stay indoors making excuses, or you can get out and get on with things.

Paul Weston presents a systematic approach to getting more out of life by guiding you through a number of easy-to-use steps.

We have two options when it comes to going for a run in the rain—stay home or get wet. This book makes it clear that rain is a poor excuse—because when it comes to *Running in the Rain—Seriously... how hard can it be?*

Purchase on Amazon
https://amzn.to/4d6Jhod

www.ingramcontent.com/pod-product-compliance
Lightning Source LLC
Chambersburg PA
CBHW071717090426
42738CB00009B/1804